SOME ASSEMBLY REQUIRED

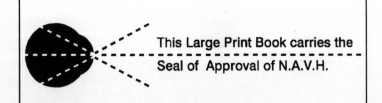

This Large Print Book carries the
Seal of Approval of N.A.V.H.

SOME ASSEMBLY REQUIRED

A JOURNAL OF MY SON'S FIRST SON

ANNE LAMOTT
WITH SAM LAMOTT

THORNDIKE PRESS

A part of Gale, Cengage Learning

GALE
CENGAGE Learning·

Detroit • New York • San Francisco • New Haven, Conn • Waterville, Maine • London

LIBRARY OF CONGRESS CATALOGING-IN-PUBLICATION DATA

Lamott, Anne.
  Some assembly required : a journal of my son's first son / by Anne Lamott with Sam Lamott.
    pages ; cm. — (Thorndike Press large print core)
    ISBN 978-1-4104-4719-7 (hardcover) — ISBN 1-4104-4719-7 (hardcover)
  1. Lamott, Anne—Family. 2. Novelists, American—20th century—Biography. I. Lamott, Sam. II. Title.
    PS3562.A4645Z46 2012b
  813'.54—dc23
  [B]   2012008136

Published in 2012 by arrangement with Riverhead Books, a member of Penguin Group (USA) Inc.

Printed in the United States of America
1 2 3 4 5 6 7 16 15 14 13 12

For Amy with profound gratitude

In the midst of the chaos
When the wind is howling I hear
the ancient song
Of the ones who went before
And know that peace will come
— SUSAN STAUTER

PREFACE
BY SAM LAMOTT

When my mother first approached me about this book, after her editor suggested the idea to her, she spoke to me over the phone in an unsure voice, her Worried Mommy voice, and her tone made me brace myself for what seemed to be a tough question. But when I realized she was asking me about whether I was okay with her writing a sequel to *Operating Instructions,* my shoulders dropped with relaxation and I shouted, "Yeah! Of course . . . Why didn't I think of that myself?" To this day, that book is the greatest gift anyone has given me; I have a very special relationship with it. When I read any of my mom's books, I hear her voice talking as if she were in the room right next to me. But when I read *Operating Instructions,* I hear and *feel* my mother's love for me, her frustration and dedication, her innermost feelings and favorite moments of my first year with her. I will always cherish these memories of our funny family and our friends, and I will always be able to come back to them, even when my mom is too old to remember them herself. (Sorry, Mom.)

Jax, when you read this one day, I want you to know the love, laughter, and endless messes of the most memorable, astonishing, and incredible year of your mother's life and mine so far. I can't wait for you to be able to understand what quirky, loving, loyal characters make up your family and friends; how much we adore you, and how much we mean to each other. It is an honor and a pleasure to be your dad; I don't know how I got so blessed to get you as my son. And I wanted you to have a book like *Operating Instructions* that is all your own.

IN THE BEGINNING

My very young son became a father in mid-July 2009, when his girlfriend, Amy Tobias, gave birth to their son. They named him Jax Jesse Lamott, Jesse after Amy's beloved grandmother Jessie, and Jax because they liked the way it sounded. Amy was twenty when she delivered, and Sam was nineteen. They're both a little young, but who asked me?

Sam's birth, on August 29, 1989, was by far the most important day of my life, and Jax's was the second. Sam and I are quite close, and I'd always looked forward with enthusiasm to becoming a grandmother someday, in, say, ten years from now, perhaps after he had graduated from the art academy he attends in San Francisco and settled down into a career, and when I was old enough to be a grandmother. I was a young fifty-five. Maybe a medium fifty-five. Let's say a ripe fifty-five, with a child just one year past his majority.

The day before Thanksgiving 2008, I had heard that Amy was expecting, when I got a call from Sam, in despair.

"Mom, I'm going to be a father," he said.

I was silent for a time. "Oh, Sam," I said finally.

He and Amy had been together, tumultuously, since his birthday a year earlier, but they had split up a couple of months before — although not, I can see now, in the biblical sense. Amy is beautiful, tiny and Hispanic, with her roots in Chicago and her parents now living in North Carolina. She had arrived in our lives on the morning of Sam's eighteenth birthday, to attend cosmetology school in San Francisco: they had become friends at a camp on the East Coast, stayed in touch by phone and text, and begun a long-term relationship, which I hadn't heard about. One day Sam told me he'd offered her his living room couch until she found an apartment. "Right," I said when he told me this plan: I was not born yesterday.

"God, Mom," he had said. Like, get your head out of the gutter.

She had moved off the couch by lunch that first day. They arrived for Sam's family party at my house at four that afternoon, very much in love. My brother Stevo, his sunny six-year-old daughter, Clara, and his fiancée, Annette, were there, as was our beloved uncle Millard, our aunt Eleanor, our best family friends, including Gertrud, a ninety-year-old German who'd always served as Sam's paternal grandmother, and a scattering of cousins. We were all transfixed by this beautiful girl who bounced into the house, in tiny shorts that would fit my cat — she is around four-foot-nine, and weighed ninety pounds at the time — with long black hair, huge brown eyes, and a perfect smile; and my first thought was, "Whom did I invite who has a teenage Hispanic daughter?" I thought she might be related to Annette, who is also Latina. Then Sam stepped inside, smiling sheepishly, and introduced Amy to me.

A little over a year later, Amy had terrible morning sickness that lasted a few months, and she spent a lot of time taking naps on my couch, and nibbling bird-sized snacks. I was happy all the time at the thought of Sam's being a father, and my getting to be a grandmother, except when I was sick with fears about their future, enraged that they had gotten themselves pregnant so young, or in a swivet of trying to control their every move, not to mention every aspect of their futures. She and Sam had moved back in together, into his tiny studio apartment on Geary, two blocks from his art school. Although Amy's parents were contributing to her expenses, I was paying Sam and Amy's rent. Amy frequently escaped to my house in Marin, mostly for companionship, as Sam was in school full-time, but also for the sun and relative peace, as their apartment was dark and loud. By the time the morning sickness passed, her belly was huge, especially because she is — or rather was — so tiny. She had an elaborate space-age ultrasound at four months, which indicated that the fetus was a boy: the technician printed out Jax's picture for us. He looked like a bright, advanced baby.

They moved into a one-room apartment a few blocks from the old studio, and created a nursery in a corner of the bedroom.

Sam was woozy with pride and scared to death. Amy was clear, calm, and fiercely into becoming a mother. She did things the way she wanted to, even when it made me unhappy. For instance, two weeks before her due date, she skipped a routine doctor's appointment for some youthful, willful reason, and I spent several days pacing around my house, trying to make peace with the idea that now the baby would almost certainly be born with some degree of disability. I cried. Sam tried to protect Amy from my neediness and anxieties — i.e., they purposely didn't call or text me for days. And they fought routinely. Amy would threaten to move back to Chicago, which made me crazier than anything, but I would not interfere, and Sam would call in despair, and I would stay neutral, with undertones of suppressed rage, and they'd come through their conflict, and I would get to be the beloved tribal elder for having stayed impartial.

We went to our little church, St. Andrew, many Sundays, unless Sam had too much homework. The month before Jax's birth, Sam was both in summer school and working for a contractor, trying to sock some money away. I had promised him a four-year education, but even though he was contributing, it was more expensive than I had expected, and I had a nagging hunch that things were not going to become cheaper after Jax was born.

I had loved being pregnant with Sam, mostly: all the parental blessings of feeling accomplished, envied, completed, astounded, proud, grateful. And I loved Amy's being pregnant with Sam's baby, mostly. I was excited that Sam was going to have all these feelings for someone, too. It would be better for him in some ways than it had been for me; I had not had any money our first few years, and that had been hard. And it could be only good for a baby to have two parents around. Yet having a child ends any feelings of complacency one might ever have, and I knew what Sam was in for. It was like having a terminal illness, but in a good way.

I frequently got to put my hands on Amy's belly and feel Jax roll and kick around in his chambers. She and I would take afternoon naps together on the two couches in my living room. She gained sixty pounds; I gained five. Her mother, Trudy, and I would get to be there at the hospital for his birth, which Amy passionately hoped to accomplish without drugs. Her mother would fly in from North Carolina near the due date, and she and I spoke or texted from time to time, making plans for Amy's hospital stay, and for just after. Amy, Sam, and the baby would come to my house from the hospital, along with Trudy, and then at some point Amy's father, Ray, would come from North Carolina to stay for a few days. We would all be one big happy family, as Ray liked to say.

I prayed every day for a healthy baby, for an easy delivery, for Sam and Amy to be good parents, and for me to let God be in charge of our lives. I prayed to be a beneficent grandmother, and not to bog down in how old that made me sound. I had two slogans to guide me. One was: *"Figure it out" is not a good slogan.* And the other was: *Ask and allow: ask God, and allow grace in.*

July 21
Amy delivered late last night by C-section after eighteen hours of hard and heroic natural labor, at the University of California San Francisco Medical Center, one of the nation's great teaching hospitals, in the upper Haight-Ashbury, just beyond the southeast corner of Golden Gate Park.

Sam had called me at two yesterday morning and told me to meet him, Amy, and Trudy at the hospital. Trudy is five-foot-six, an inch shorter than I am, brunette, and very sweet, a few years older than I. Her grandma nomenclature will be "Grammy," and mine will be "Nana," which is what Sam called my mother. Amy was given a private room, and was plugged into various monitors. Sam coached her for the first few hours, and then Trudy and I coached her, and then Sam again. After many hours, Amy was dilated to six centimeters, but she wasn't getting any further. She refused any drugs for hours, even Pitocin to intensify the contractions, and watching her I felt crazy with powerlessness and thwarted Good Ideas: Let's everyone settle down and take a lot of drugs! Get this show on the road! Of course, I pretended to be supportive of whatever she decided. Sam, Trudy, and I took turns going to the cafeteria for snacks, while Amy was brought hospital meals which no one ate, because the meals looked like upscale pet food, with a side of boiled vegetables. When all was said and done, we ate mostly Cheetos and M&M's. And when I say "we," I mean me.

Amy's contractions were wracking her body, but they weren't quite productive enough. She was in maternal warrior mode, and I was humbled by how hard she was working, how much pain she was able to bear, and how stoic she was. By this point in my own labor, almost twenty years before, I'd already had the Pitocin, an epidural, and a few refreshing shots of morphine to take the edge off. I felt stunned and teary about what a good birth coach Sam was — it wasn't so long ago that we were bickering about wet towels on the bathroom floor or why the hell he can't manage to keep his cell phone charged.

Hours later, Amy finally let the nurses put

some Pitocin in her IV, and the three of us took turns breathing with her. But the baby, who had been estimated to weigh nine pounds, was just too big for her small body, and she was exhausted. At seven that night, a number of doctors came by on rounds, with third-year medical students in tow, and said, Tut-tut, like Pooh in the Hundred Acre Wood, and then that everything looked fine — and finally, at around eight or so, a doctor who looked a lot like a young Ethel Kennedy, scrappy and beautiful, bounded in, as if we were all on a tennis court. She was about my age and she exuded intelligence, and we all instantly knew she was perfect — although her eyes squinted like a mole would in sudden bright sun. My first thought was, "Oh my God, she's a blind gynecologist. Affirmative action has gone too far this time." There were so many nurses in the room, with a few scattered leftover med students thrown in, and a new batch of med students. Within a minute, Dr. Ethel had most of her arm inside Amy.

All of us held our collective breath when she said, "Oh, *jeez,* is that the umbilical cord?" and some of the medical students and the labor nurse made the quiet face of studious, hopeful concern that nurses are taught in their first semester. And then the doctor said cheerfully, "Oh, it's just an ear." Like, Silly me! Sighs of relief all around. Then her arm disappeared again, up to her elbow, as if she could wiggle her fingers and tickle Amy's heart. She squinted off to one side, way in the distance, as if to the hills whence help comes, like Mr. Magoo in Pharaoh's Egypt, and I realized she was not seeing with her eyes, but with her hand and her mind. As I watched her bend in, with her head and shoulders sideways, I was reminded of all those times as children when we stretched sideways over a storm drain, an ear pressed against the grille, reached our arms through, and blindly tried to grab a coin from below with our fingertips, before resorting to sticking a wad of bubble gum on the end of a stick.

Finally the doctor's arm reappeared, and she explained to Amy that there was way too much amniotic fluid, which posed a dangerous hurdle, and she needed to break Amy's water. We all nodded knowingly, even the medical students. The labor nurse gave the doctor a needle, and the doctor's arm disappeared again, and after a minute she announced that she had pierced the sac and would let the water out slowly.

But the water gushed out of Amy, about ten gallons of a green soup from *The Exor-*

cist, and I thought with my ever-present Christian faith: Amy's dying now for sure; I just hope they can save the baby. But the doctor squinted at the hills again and repositioned the baby's arm and hand; she was, we learned later, trying to keep the rivers of soup from pouring over the sides of the banks all at once: she was siphoning it off.

Amy lay in a widening pool of green soupy fluid; nurses tried to shove towels under her butt without bumping the now one-armed doctor. The doctor's head tilted, in full squint; she worked on until she seemed to listen for a minute, but not with her visible ears. Then she withdrew her arm and took off the glove.

She told Amy that she would give her one more hour, but she didn't think there was a big chance of success, even with more Pitocin. Amy should have a C-section, while there was still a choice. I was silently begging, *Please* have it. Amy looked to Sam, and he told her that it was her body, that he supported her in whatever she decided. I wanted to scream into his face, "Stop saying that! You're *encouraging* her," but somehow I didn't say anything. Amy asked for more Pitocin, yet an hour later when the nurse checked her cervix, she said it was

21

just the same. She left the room, and the four of us prayed together as a family. After a few minutes, Dr. Ethel came back, and her arm disappeared up Amy again. In full Mole Squint, the doctor said, "I recommend we do a cesarean," and Amy said, quietly, "Okay."

Trudy and I went off to the waiting room, where we writhed around and read the sacred texts of crisis — *People* and the *National Enquirer* — and ate the temple foods — Cheetos and M&M's — for about an hour, until a huge male nurse came to tell us that Jax had been born. Amy was fine, but she desperately needed to sleep for a few hours, before she could begin nursing. He said we could go meet the baby. Trudy and I hugged and jumped and pumped our grandmotherly fists.

We found Sam in the nursery, dressed in scrubs, holding his swaddled new son, peering into his peaceful face, crying and saying over and over, "Hi Jax, I'm your dad. I'm your dad, Jax."

Jax was the loveliest baby boy I've ever seen, a dead ringer for Sam as a newborn, but Latino, gorgeous as God or a crescent moon, with huge black eyes, nearly black hair, lightly tan. I felt as though I was seeing a river gorge, from way up high on a bridge, silenced by the vastness of his tiny face, the depth of his brown-black eyes.

July 22–23

Amy is much better, even though she is still in great pain, and Sam is madly in love with Jax and doing a good job taking care of both him and Amy. Trudy is here for two weeks, staying at the kids' apartment in the city until they come to my house for a week. We are together all day, every day, at UC Med. Trudy is a social worker in real life. She's down-to-earth, outgoing, and constantly doing something useful. Everyone is exhausted beyond all imagining, especially Amy and Sam.

The best thing — besides how unbelievably perfect Jax is, not to mention alive — is to watch Sam be a father. He stayed up with Jax in the nursery the whole first night, holding him. Jax takes naps on Sam on the pull-out bed, which is more of a padded bench, and the three will be there in Amy's room until Friday afternoon, when they come to my house. Then Amy's father will fly in to join us. I am ever so slightly concerned, since I spend ninety percent-plus of my time alone with the animals, that having all of these people around will be overwhelming, and slightly tiring, but this is life on life's terms, not Annie's.

Jax has pouty lips, and a Mongolian spot right at the top of his bottom. It is bruise-blue, common to ethnic babies; fifty percent or so of Latin American babies have the spot. The Japanese call it the "blue butt." These birthmarks usually disappear in a few years. He also has one on his instep, the size of a nickel, like a thumbprint.

I can't capture how it feels to watch Sam change poopy diapers. He uses several wipes, then takes one last wipe and says, "Time for the final shine," and polishes Jax up.

July 22
Tom is one of Sam's and my oldest friends. He's a Jesuit, renowned throughout the country for his spiritual lectures and retreats. He is larger than life, one paradox after another: He is by turns loquacious and taciturn. He takes over most rooms that he enters, but he's also the best listener I know. Educated to within an inch of his life, sober thirty years, with a sense of humor that is irreverent, self-effacing, and wise. He lives in Oakland with four other Jesuits and some cats. We have traveled with him all over the world since Sam was two. He looks like an aging radical hippie in his Australian sun

hats; he is often surrounded by people who hang on his every word, like followers. He is cherished, hilarious, and difficult, and Sam considers it one of my few achievements to have lured Tom into being close friends with me.

Sam sent me the following e-mail tonight:

"I had asked Tom to visit us at the hospital, partly to see and bless my new son, because he's a priest, but it was also really about wanting to *give* him to my friend, Kenny Boo. I'd arranged for Kenny to come see Jax at the same time as Tom, because Kenny is also a new father. But because he is black, the road will be much harder for him. This is just true, and he needs to know a guy like Tom, who is the most brilliant man on earth, spiritually and in book ways. Also, I love that you can ask him anything about history, and he'll know.

"Tom has always been such a loving friend, and I was sure Kenny would think he was a trip. You'd never know he was a Jesuit most of the time, because he is sort of scruffy, but if you talk to him, and see especially how he listens so closely, you know he is a man of God. He is important to my story, as I have looked up to him since I was two, and he was the first person I asked to come see us.

25

"This visit was nothing short of wondrous to me. Kenny Boo, a six-foot-eight-inch friend who is scary to a lot of people but is actually a teddy bear, meeting Tom, looking kind of gone-to-seed in an aging-guru way, in a Hawaiian shirt in the foggy city, and a panama hat. This visit was so special because I had two of my closest people visiting me: the most educated older guy I know, I mean, right up there with Millard, and then someone like me who barely got through high school. They were the only people I asked to come to the hospital, because I trust them in the deepest blood way. They are brothers to me.

"I was looking forward to Tom's arrival because I wanted Kenny to see what somebody looking through life with the eyes of God looks like. Kenny and his girlfriend had a son two months ago, and their life is pretty hard. Usually wherever Kenny goes, he has to see people react to how gigantic and dark he is, but Tom was one person who would not project this onto him.

"I already knew I could count on Tom's consistent, unconditional love to come into play here, even though he is not a father. Well, he *is* a Father, but does not have children. I remember him telling you when I was young that he would have been better at raising reptiles than kids.

"When Tom showed up, Kenny was already there. Tom gave us both big welcoming hugs, even though I was the host, spoke to us like he was already brothers with Kenny, and drew us into crazy discussions — about Costco, the Bible, and Costco Bibles.

"Mom, I think you remember how angry I was at both of you (you and Trudy) because you guys were making everything all about yourselves. I also needed the car keys in Trudy's pocket, but you two were so chattery and nervous that I couldn't get this across to you. I felt like I might go crazy.

"Tom totally stayed out of the energy. He just stood there as if he was basically uninterested, but then when you and Trudy left, he held a space for me to really go off on you guys. Then he pulled me back in, to just him and me, once I was finished. He said: 'Breathe. Keep it simple. My mother has driven me crazy for sixty years.' "

July 24–August 1, Home with the Baby
It has been high energy at my usually dull, quiet house. Jax; Sam and Amy, who sometimes bicker, and who are vaporous and otherworldly with fatigue; Trudy, on a mattress in the kitchen nook; and the two big dogs

and the cat, who is bitter. Jax mostly sleeps, nurses, poops, blinks at you with black goggle eyes, pees on you while you are changing him, passes out. Amy's mom is social and talkative, which is hard for me because I am usually just with myself all day. Trudy and Amy don't always get along. It is a pretty typical mother-daughter situation. Amy and Sam have huge needs for food, laundry, sometimes companionship, often isolation, but don't always know which, so it is exhausting to tiptoe around if they are not getting along, or to get dismissed, even when I am in my loveliest, least intrusive, most saintly mode.

It is crowded and fraught here sometimes — as if everyone has PMS at once, including Jax, and tiny Amy with these now gigantic 36G breasts, often exposed, and I get sick of seeing them, as she is frequently topless in their room because Jax nurses so much and her bra hurts her nipples, and under stress, I become *National Geographic*-averse. I don't even especially like Sam's going around without a shirt on. I want to shout, "Everyone must have clothes on when he or she is in my hut! And please use the forks, which you'll find in the basket in the center of the table."

Other times, it's easy village living, Trudy

and I happily doing housework together a lot, Amy nursing the baby every two hours, all of us changing these truly disgusting mustardy diapers from the black lagoon. I remember thinking when Sam was newborn: How can this magical precious being produce such *filth?* I used to wonder if Sam was doing this out of baby spite, taking my glorious milk and turning it into such a foul product. And how could such voluminous waste come out of such a tiny vessel? It would be as if a newborn kitten shat a whole haggis.

Yesterday I was walking around the house with Jax, who was sleeping in my arms, and we really were the ultimate portrait of what heaven will be like. But when we came into Amy and Sam's bedroom, they were fighting about whether to separate or not. Just then I wished I had a gun so Jax and I could shoot our way out of this messy situation, and then I remembered: Oh, wait — *they're* the parents. Rats.

So I transformed myself into Red Cross Field Station Management Nurse, and mobilized Amy, Trudy, and Jax for his first stroller walk to the redwood park. That was lovely, and great for Sam to have a little space, but I felt the burden of the fight and our exhaustion. The small children on the structures at the park looked like linebackers and Slavs compared with Jax.

I sneaked out that night, to be alone in the car, with the radio off and a bag of medicinal chocolate, although I had already gained four pounds in the hospital cafeteria during our stay, and felt like a fat old granny. When I got back home, Sam was mean to me because I had forgotten to buy cereal, and Amy was mad at Trudy for talking too much, so Trudy and I sat on the couch together, with blankies and my leftover chocolates, and binged on legal shows.

Through it all, though, the ups and downs, Jax shines like a pearl.

Looking at Sam's and Amy's faces when they hold him, so madly in love, and watching Sam changing poopy diapers all the time nearly brings me to tears. My wild son, who like most boys smashed and bashed his way through childhood, with branches and bats and wooden swords, who shut down and pulled so far away as a teenager that sometimes I could not find him, now taking tender care of his own newborn, a miniature who is both unique and reflective. Sam is still every age he ever was, from the fetus to the infant to the adolescent to the father. And Einstein would probably say that Jax is already every age he will ever be, but in such super-slow motion relative to our limited perspective that we can't see the full spiral of him yet, only this tan bundle of perfect infanthood with a blue butt.

One night I ran away from home and told everyone I was going to Bible study at St. Andrew, but instead I went to Macy's. I tried to shell out money on something really meaningless and bourgeois, like blusher or overpriced Peds, but I was too screwed up mentally. Or too well; I'm not sure. Couldn't find one thing to buy, so I sat in the parking lot, enraged, bereft, empty, fit to be tied, watching the bad movie in what my spiritual mentor Bonnie calls Theater B. Theater A is where we see goodness in everything, beauty and generosity or, conversely, someone's need for love. Theater B is where I watch a movie about how this exquisite baby could ruin Sam's academic career, if the baby even lives, and how Sam would end up at the rescue mission and so on. *Finally* I thought to pray — it had completely escaped me that I believe in divine mind and comfort. I'd forgotten that if I said the Great Prayer — Help — I would experience that God was with me, that, as Muktananda put it, God dwells within me, *as* me. And that Mother Teresa would have seen me as Jesus, in His distressing guise as OCD

Grandma, worthy of tenderness. So I broke bread with myself, with a health food oat biscuit I had in my purse, and a paper cup of water from an earlier stealth binge at Taco Bell. I called my dearest male friend, Doug, who lives in Chicago. He made cooing sounds as I described how hard it could be at home right now, and he reminded me of his new battle cry: *Lower the bar of expectations!* I'd forgotten. After we got off the phone, I flew home, in love again with my peeps.

July 29–31

My baby brother Stevo turns fifty today. He is six-foot-three now, so I am not able to hold him and lug him around as I did until I was ten and he was five. My memories of holding him when my parents brought him home from the hospital are as sharp and clear as can be. I have an old photo of me holding newborn Stevo on the couch of our little coffee-colored house, sitting with our older brother, John, and I am crying. I remember that my parents were exasperated with me for crying on this happiest day, but now I think I felt heartbroken because at five years old, I understood what this baby boy was in for. Fresh, and doomed, to be born human at all, let alone into this miserable marriage. He has been my great secret advantage ever since.

Ray arrived today at one from North Carolina for a four-day visit. I've met him before, for dinners and at events to celebrate Amy's graduation from cosmetology school in San Francisco. He is in his mid-sixties, close to six feet tall; spiritual and outgoing, he works out and is a health nut, but always tan — which to me, the daughter of a man who died of melanoma, is a contradiction in terms. He's bald on top, with the sides buzz-cut, and he seems like a farmer type from the South. Amy once described him as "ruggedy." I think she meant "rugged," but she perfectly captured his rugged raggedy-ness. His glasses were duct-taped the first time we met, and Amy tells me that duct tape and Gorilla Glue are his two favorite products. He Gorilla Glues his shoe soles when they start to go.

He describes himself as having been a preacher, teacher, cop, and monk.

My favorite Ray story is that when Amy went to visit him last year, he came to the breakfast table without his bottom dentures. When Amy commented, he blew it off, saying, "Oh, we're in the South. No one cares."

I would love to see this guy at church for an hour every week, but having him and

Trudy, Sam, Amy, and Jax in my house is one of the hardest things I've ever done. Everyone absolutely rose to the occasion, but Amy and Trudy rubbed on each other's nerves in such small quarters, and Ray prepared a salad big enough for a hundred people, which under the circumstances made me want to hit him — you're using up ALL my salad vegetables, Mr. Gorilla-Glued Soles. Amy hid out in her room most of the time, often without her shirt on, still needing to feed Jax every two hours. Sam was in basic catatonia, begging for errands to do so he could get in the car and leave.

Trudy and Ray were calm and uncomplaining about living so far from their grandson, even as it was obvious that this would be hard for them. I noted and appreciated this. Half the time we were lovely together, the six of us — SIX of us, wow. And that was some kind of miracle, that we pulled it off at all, the three grandparents tending to this marvelous baby and the two erratic young parents: keeping healthy meals coming, laundry washed and folded, sobbing baby swaddled and walked and rocked to sleep. Trudy and I moved beyond *Law & Order,* which turned out to be a gateway drug to an even more addictive new legal series on TV that we hooked into obsessively, sometimes watching two or three episodes a night. We also walked the dogs. We used them as an excuse to leave every few hours and go up the old fire road to the shady glade nearby. The poor dogs lost weight, and maybe got blisters, for all I know.

I was so exhausted by having to have long small-talk conversations with everyone all day that I sneaked from room to room like an agent for Mossad, just trying to find a moment's space, just trying to find, as Ram Dass put it forty years ago, my heart cave. I tiptoed past the bedrooms, through the living room, then, like Rubber Girl, stretched around the corner from the dining room, past Trudy and Ray's bedroom in the kitchen nook, to my office.

August 1

The six of us had a sweet last morning together. I was in a great mood, because we had pulled it off. (And because they were all leaving.) While everyone packed up, I held Jax, and tried to memorize the smell of his skin, that alert face, the dark stub of his umbilical cord. It's a tiny, pumpkinish stem.

They headed to Sam and Amy's apartment on Geary, except for Trudy, who will fly back to North Carolina. The silence and space here are lovely, like a redwood forest — and I miss everyone already and have no purpose in life. I guess things will return to normal, whatever that means now.

August 2

Sam surprised me by bursting into church alone, right as it was starting, in a religious fever of needing to escape from Amy, Jax, and Ray, who was leaving on the red-eye that night. Our pastor Veronica made a big fuss from the pulpit about Sam's joy, and the arrival of our newest brother, and Sam promised to bring him and Amy next week. About fifteen minutes into the service, he started missing Jax in that aching physical way, almost like a nursing mother. He is so doomed. So he went and snagged Isaiah, who is a year older than Jax, and whom Sam and I refer to as his training baby — he has been holding him every Sunday for months, and watched his parents, Kim and Dominick, diaper, burp, and cuddle with him. They have promised Amy and Sam all of Isaiah's hand-me-downs.

Sam held Isaiah so differently from how he did even a month ago, because his hands have become the hands of a father.

I heard him whisper to Isaiah, "Cool shoes, dude," and then he leaned over to me, waggling his eyebrows conspiratorially, and said, "Jax will look *great* in these."

My heart was broken today in the best way, watching people cry with Sam about his blessing, having held him and fought for possession of him nearly twenty years ago. This church has prayed us through everything — his birth; his worst asthma attacks; starting school; meeting his father, John, at age seven; then all those scary visits to see him in Vancouver; puberty; and the hard teenage times when we nearly lost it some days. There are fewer of us now at church, fifty or so most Sundays, but it is pretty much as it has been since Sam was born. It's a kitchen church, not a church-on-display, all these black and white and brown people who need and want to be here. And it is the same as when I first came in, twenty-five years ago, hungover and bulimic, weighing twenty pounds less than I do now, when I could stay because they didn't rush me, like a sorority, or try to get me to believe.

The people saw that I was in pain, and they let me be; and they let me be with them, and let me find Him the best I could.

Today people shuffled in, happy and relieved to be there, disappointed that Sam hadn't brought Jax, but crowding around me during the Passing of the Peace to see the photos on my cell phone — my screen picture is of Sam holding Jax and staring into his brand-new face. At St. Andrew, there are all levels of shyness and grand public display during the Peace, but somehow every one of them is a hug of recognition, which is all that most of us need or want, in a kind of churchly square dance, hand to hand to hand.

The hymns are bigger than any mistakes; you fumble around with the hymnal and sing the wrong words — sometimes I'm on the wrong verse — but the hymn expands to make room for each voice, even yours. We speak as a body; we have set the intent together, so rather than individual shrill cries or drones of one crazy person, it's a braid.

August 3, E-mail from Sam
Me in general
1. Powerless — trying to be comfortable in utter powerlessness. Not strong suit.
2. My opinion is meaningless — can only offer body for service. Verbal input useless; just really have to trust Amy, and her intuition.
3. Hate both of these things.

Hi, Mom. Here's the skinny on the fam: Jax's fingernails have gotten long again; we clipped them just last week. This is already one of our least favorite things to do. Since last night, he's managed to scratch his face a couple of times badly. A new development is that now when we pick him up, even if he is swaddled, he flails his arms in the air, instead of lying passively in baby burrito mode. His hands now open and close, and because he is armed with claws, he scratches everything — including us.

Between feedings last night, he was trying to stay awake with us, which was throwing off our schedule, because he needs to sleep, we need to rest, and then he needs to eat again often, every three hours. It's like a perpetual motion machine. We loved it at the time last night, because it was so cute to just look at him. Now, however, we are all wasted.

I remember the first time I looked into his eyes, two weeks ago, it felt like staring into a sky full of space, but the size of a marble. Or into a deep tiny ocean. We enjoyed our awake time with him until it caught up to us and he was both exhausted and hungry at once. He wanted to eat but was too tired to fully latch on, and was sobbing because it meant he couldn't get milk.

Amy is exhausted from Jax being fussy all night because of the frustrating sleeping/eating situation. I took Jax and let her sleep in, but she isn't pumping her breast milk so I can't feed him. This makes me sad and mad, not to sound too much like a Dr. Seuss book.

I started thinking about how much I really hate the umbilical cord stump and wish I could pick it off. I'm fantasizing about how much easier life will be without it — bathing, being able to throw on diapers without worrying about it. This damn stump has been a nightmare for someone who worries and likes to control things, because it has been spotty, bloody, and not at all cooperating with what I'd like to see there, which is a nice plain tummy.

But as I was writing this just now, Jax began to fuss. I walked over to pick him up, and as I did, this black thing rolls off him. I quickly realized it's the stump! I should be like, "Hooray," right?

Nope. As I was going over to show off the new stomach situation to Amy, who has been peacefully sleeping, I looked down at where the stump was, and I was now con-

40

vinced that I could see his insides.

I don't think it healed right, and I'm looking at what must be his large intestine! I woke Amy up in a panic, yelling at her to call the paramedics — Jax needs surgery. Amy looks at what I'm seeing and is very concerned but somehow keeps her cool and calls the pediatrician. During the phone call, I find *blood* on his fingernails. I've caught him red-handed — he has clawed open his stomach. Plus it's all our fault because we didn't clip his nails.

Amy called the pediatrician's office, and nobody seemed to be concerned that my baby's guts were coming out of his stomach. I mean the person on the phone, and then the advice nurse who listened to our concerns. There was no emotional change on their part.

Are these people desensitized?

When I'm convinced my child is dying, the medical professionals trying to sound calm actually have the opposite effect for me. So on the phone, I feel that this is a dire emergency, and my baby probably needs emergency surgery, so these receptionists and nurses should be *very* attentive and concerned. Instead, they gently convince us that we didn't even need to come in! That Jax was perfectly fine. This small open wound turned out to be just a normal old gooey belly button. They see it every day.

We covered it up with a SpongeBob SquarePants Band-Aid. All is well, ish.

August 4

Amy's two best friends, Amanda and Michelle, drove all the way from Chicago to see her and meet the baby. They are staying at the apartment in San Francisco. They are both lovely in every way. The three of them are so young, children really, who have been together since childhood. They came over today with Jax to visit me, and I plunged into feeling less-than. They are beautiful, lively, have strong backs, and a lot more energy than I am going to see again. They are the main reason Amy sometimes talks about wanting to move back to Chicago, along with her grandmother Nonny, Trudy's mother, who is in a home, with advanced dementia and heart failure. Other relatives live there, too, lots of cousins and aunts and uncles with whom she is close; everyone but her parents. Amanda and Michelle are gaga over the baby, cuckoo for Cocoa Puffs, and Amy gets to be a girl again, instead of stuck in the wife-and-mother role.

Amanda is going to be Jax's godmother, although there have been no discussions about his baptism. I assume and hope that he will be baptized at St. Andrew when he is three months old, as Sam was. I drove them out to Samuel P. Taylor State Park, one of my favorite places on earth, and gave them the Annie California History Tour. They are so much fun that I started feeling competitive again. I am old and unfun. Amy hates it when I even joke about seeing them as the competition, or as my contenders — but at breakfast, when I tried to sic the dogs on them, Amanda and Michelle both thought it was funny.

They were taking pictures of one another at the park, and I took pictures of them holding Jax, and standing inside the burnt-out trunk of a giant redwood. How can Sam and I possibly compete with these two young women, Sam who fights with Amy sometimes, and me with my CIA Black Ops attempts to get Amy to need me so much that she has to stay here forever? And get a job? Oh, wait, just remembered — it's not a competition. Ah. Got it. Roger. Copy that.

August 6, E-mail from Amy
Today, me and the girls and Jax of course went to Fisherman's Wharf. After finally

parking, the clock in my head told me that Jax had one hour of sleep left before his next feeding time. I didn't want to go too far from the car, because since I had a c-section, my uterus still really hurts, and I can't nurse him the traditional way — it hurts — I have to hold him football style. Also I'm like a dairy farm with too many cows. I never run out of milk. I swear. I'm constantly leaking, especially at feeding time — the side that is unoccupied doesn't just drip while it's waiting its turn — it's more like a waterfall pouring out. Nursing in public is complicated. My system when I'm out is to go to the car, set up the changing table, stuff a towel in one side of my bra, grab him and position him like a football and hold him up. I know this sounds complicated — it is — but it works.

Anyway, we're making our way down Fisherman's Wharf, farther and farther away from the car, 'cause I am just starved for this sort of normal friendship thing. And to my surprise Jax is sleeping overtime. He has now been asleep for two and a half hours, when I thought he only had one hour left. We get to the very end of the wharf, and all of us are so hungry, but since I was making tacos for dinner, we decide to settle for a Ben & Jerry's ice cream cone. Well, the line was *extremely* long and not moving, and I was losing hope and trying to keep Jax asleep with my willpower, and finally, finally, I order my double scoop of mint chocolate chip ice cream in a waffle cone. I'm dying of starvation and worn-out from all the walking, so we sit down to enjoy our ice cream, and it was heaven. Then I get *exactly* two licks of this overly great treat when Michelle says, "I think Jax is crying." My first reaction is, "No, I don't hear anything," because the thought of not eating this ice cream is just too sad. But yup, Jax has started to cry. He woke up and now wants to eat, and yes of course he has a terrible dirty diaper, too. I just hand Amanda my ice cream to throw out, sigh, pick up Jax from the stroller so he will be calm, and we rush all the way back to the car, with him screaming, all poopy and miserable, and the girls looking everywhere for a public bathroom, any public bathroom, but no luck.

We finally find a place. Then we make it to the car after almost three hours since we arrived. I change him, nurse him, and then have to change him *again* just while we're sitting there. On the way home, for the first time ever, Jax stayed awake in the car. I was giving Amanda and Michelle the tour of San Francisco, and asked Michelle, who was sit-

45

ting next to Jax in the backseat, if he was sleeping, and she said, "Nope, he's just looking out the window," but he was not crying. He was just looking out the window at San Francisco. It was like he was listening. It was the first time he's stayed awake in the car without crying.

August 8

My life would be infinitely harder if my mother were alive, because she was impossible, and then sick with Alzheimer's, but I'm sad that she didn't get to know Jax. She and Sam loved each other deeply until her death, when he was eleven. She appreciated him in a way she wasn't able to do with her three kids. Kids are hard — they drive you crazy and break your heart — whereas grandchildren make you feel great about life, and yourself, and your ability to love someone unconditionally, finally, after all these years. A friend of mine said, "When I return, I am only having grandchildren, not children." A grandchild is like a fine jewel set in an old ring.

Sam's other grandmother, Gertrud, was by appointment, not blood: I asked her about six weeks after he was conceived to be Sam's paternal grandmother, since his father, John, was not involved. Besides,

Sam's real paternal grandmother had died years before. Gertrud had been my mother's best friend for thirty-five years when Sam was born, and her children, with whom we had grown up, could see that she loved Sam in a much more exuberant and pure way than she had loved them. She died in late 2008, and that broke Sam's heart for a long time, but she lived long enough to be close to Amy. This was where I got to see Amy's profound way with older people, which I think is her greatest gift, and which I try to remember when she is pushing my buttons. She always showed up to help care for Gertrud, and was like an Egyptian servant girl to her, all but fanning her with palm fronds. She went to Gertrud's house when she was an invalid, and gave her haircuts, manicures, and pedicures, which was exactly what Gertrud needed and wanted but couldn't ask for, because she felt both too proud and too ashamed. She had been such a beautiful woman. Amy gave her shampoos, filed and painted the bad toenails until they were pretty again, rubbed lotion into her ancient arms and legs, practically changed water into wine.

Amy helped Gertrud have beauty again in that wracked and ruined body. What price can you possibly put on that? I remember

47

this all the time and am grateful.

Life is mostly okay right now, sometimes lovely and peaceful; and when it's not, it's hard and weird for my nineteen-year-old son to have a baby, and the scary parts feel like they could break you. But then those parts pass, against all odds, and things are mostly okay again, temporarily. Until they get hard and weird again and break your heart. It's not a great system. If I were God's West Coast rep, I'd come up with something easier, whose outcome you could bank on.

August 8

I was trying to be gracious with Amy while simultaneously manipulating her today over the phone, attempting to maneuver her toward setting a future date to go look for a job. She was quiet and unresponsive. Another way of saying that is: She did not take the bait. I like to think of what I am doing as "helping her get back to her career path," although she has not worked since graduating from cosmetology school, six months ago. I actually thought that I was trying to impart my truth, which is that everybody has to work. But I think she sees me as chirpy, intrusive, and judgmental, which, while she is probably right, still hurts my feelings.

I am having a hard time. I'm lonely and between books and boyfriends, although "between" suggests there are new ones waiting on the other side of these doldrums. So, since I am without a plan — or, for that matter, much of a future — the uneasiness of the world has been creeping in, and I was feeling peculiar and odd. And then Amy called a while later to say that she and Jax missed me, and were coming for a visit.

I sort of clutched one hand to my chest in a swoon. Saved by the bell.

Jax has the most fabulous hair, dark, defined, and sculpted by baby sweat; it's elegant while easygoing, in a gangsterish way.

He's gained back the weight he lost in the first few days of life, and he is now at least ten pounds, with the tawny skin of a ripe peach. He is all health and life and delectability — life force with earth in it, Mayan life force, like his mother.

I especially love tracing the outline of his eyebrows. They are already so strong, like a photo developing slowly.

You fall into his eyes because he looks like he's taking things in with great concentration. He has a very nice nose, definitely Amy's nose, ever so slightly wider than

Sam's. Although, of course, very seldom does a baby not have a charming nose. Besides, it's not what you concentrate on.

His face becomes a wide screen when he's wrapped up in a blanket, and it flickers, flutters, when he sleeps. Then he smiles, but it's digestive stuff, although *not* according to Sam, who says it is love, which is what my late, great best friend Pammy always said about Sam's first smiles. He has a great crooked grin, whether that is gas or delight, and then an old man's worried concentration. His expression shifts so fast, as though he's trying on all the stuff in the bag of facial muscles and expressions.

Sam has the same quality as Jax, as if something full of wonder has fallen out of the sky; there are times when they both look transcendent and dazed. Their eyes are huge, brown, and unfathomable. He and Jax, and Jax and Amy, pour into each other the connection and communion like a palpable thrum of energy and fear and marvel.

I've never seen Sam so there: all his humor and lightness and joshing and focus. It's like, "He's my baby and I can kind of sort of take care of him." I am spellbound as Sam holds him, sits with him — meditative activity that is otherwise hard for a nineteen-year-old.

Amy is holding on to Jax for dear life. She is still hurting, and I think she needs the constant flesh connection to soothe the pain. She's the tender bar. Sam seems glad for every break that Amy's time with Jax gives him; he picks up sketchbooks and zones out on his art.

Me, I'm the worry-wart. I think this is a public service, so that Sam and Amy can relax. When I carry Jax in a sling, I want to check his vital signs every few minutes, maybe do a little prophylactic CPR.

Sam and Amy are often at their best, with stoic pride and joy and solidarity and endless hard work, but Sam gets to be much lighter about everything, because he's not the mother. Amy's a cavewoman, sitting in the hut. It's easy for Sam to get out in the sun or take off in the car, because he doesn't have to lug around milk jugs, or the physical pain. Amy's sequestered in the cave. She's an achy vessel. She has to move with care. She has to hold herself the way she holds the baby. She's very focused, very workmanlike; she has a job to do, and nothing is going to stop her. She's pumping milk to relieve the pressure in her breasts, but Sam says she does not seem willing to let him give Jax this milk in bottles very often.

51

Of course, this is his side of the story. I don't have a clue what their private life is really like. I assume she does most of the work, because Sam is a full-time student, and — this will sound judgmental, but I say it with love — the male. She says it's better for Jax to nurse exclusively, but I don't agree, when there is a father in the picture. I nursed until Sam was thirteen months, but early on, I pumped milk frequently so that Pammy, Stevo, my mom, Gertrud, and Sam's unofficial Big Brother Brian could give him nourishment, too. They were like his composite father. I love hearing about fathers who get up in the middle of the night to give an infant a bottle of breast milk. But maybe the truth is that Sam is lazy about helping. She and Sam fight about it, because the plan had been for Sam to share feeding duties, and I had loved this idea — and to this end, Amy had asked me for an extremely expensive breast pump, which I provided. But as my favorite joke says, if you want to make God laugh, tell Her your plans.

Still, I pretend to be beatific in my neutrality. I let them flail it out, because that is the sort of caring soul I am.

Nature is trying to help them define themselves in this new way. They are remaking who they are, at a core level, with a third. Whereas before, sometimes they didn't do all that well as two. And now three, our fabulous new person dumped into the middle of a tough relationship.

August 9, E-mail from Amy
Sorry it is so hard for me to write to you, we are both sick with tiredness most of the time. I loved our first time together at St. Andrew today, how everyone cried with being happy. When Sam stood up while holding him and said, "This is our son," it was like *The Lion King,* and we both cried, but luckily Jax didn't, 'cause he was asleep.

And tonight, he had his first bath. You could tell he was very content 'cause he peed very casually, like lah lah lah, just going pee in my bath with my mom and dad.

August 11, E-mail from Amy
Jax is a sucker. Even when he's not hungry, all he wants to do is suck. Sometimes we'll try to give him a binky, but when he falls asleep, it'll fall out, and then when he tries to suck again, it wakes him up 'cause he's mad it's gone. So we usually resort to giving him our finger. But tonight more than once he found his thumb and was in total ecstasy.

I am going to take Jax to visit my parents in the next few weeks. They are going to meet us in Chicago so all my aunts and uncles and cousins and best friends can see him (us) too.

August 13
My uncle Millard stopped by to meet Jax today, and to see Sam and pay homage, as he put it, to Amy. He lives right up the street with his son Ricky and his grandson Oliver, who has just become a teenager. Millard and I have lunch every two or three weeks, and Sam, Stevo, and I cannot get enough of him. He is the patriarch of the family, the husband of fifty years to my mother's twin sister, Pat. He is in his mid-eighties and has been a father figure to my brothers and me since our father died; Millard often tells stories about my father, his brother-in-law, with whom he was great friends. He is, or used to be, the same height as my father, six-foot-one, and has always been skinny, even though he is a gourmet chef, cooking constantly, and now I think he is down to about 125 pounds since my aunt Pat's death. He has small, quick, brown eyes and a skinny chiseled face, a finely strung Jewish scholar's face, and beautiful teeth that are sort of incongruous — a lovely smile. He is

up there with the two or three smartest people I know, a history professor for years at the College of Marin, with a deep vein of spirituality that he insists be borne up by his understanding of science, and what can be proven, and especially how it might dovetail with what modern physics could prove.

Sam loves him more than any other man except Stevo. He asked Millard to be a grandfather to Jax, but Millard told him, "Oh, sweetheart, I just want to be the very best great-uncle once removed, or great-great-uncle, or whatever the hell it is I would be."

Millard hugged and kissed Amy and me at the door, and tiptoed into the living room in case Jax was sleeping, but he wasn't. So Millard sat down next to Sam and took Jax out of his arms, and gave him the big Shalom — it is *always* the big Shalom with Millard, the big skinny welcome, the bagelly Shalom, not Moses and not schmaltzy, but tribal, the chief coming by to welcome the newest brother.

August 15
I'm trying not to think about Amy and Jax going to Chicago. It will be hard not seeing him for a few weeks, but I often think of

Trudy and Ray, who have to go for months between visits, and this helps me to be less of a whiny baby than I would otherwise be. This is the one fly in the grandma ointment — the total love addiction — the highest highs, and then withdrawal, craving, scheming to get another fix. All I do is wait for another chance to be with the baby. He has basically ruined my life. I begin to think about Jax the moment I wake up, wondering what he can do now that he couldn't do yesterday. But it is not my fault — we're wired to be delighted, obsessed; we're engineered that way.

Babies' smells set off chemical reactions through us that make us want to love and nurture them. This is such an unfair advantage, and it is truly how they get you. What if al-Qaeda could weaponize this?

Where else will you see someone who is *never* mean, or who isn't wrecked yet? By kindergarten, almost all kids have gone a little bad, because so many families are unhealthy and competition to succeed starts so early — way before kindergarten nowadays. For Jax, at nearly a month, nothing is wrecked. His skin is so ethereal and smooth, and he is not required to do anything or make decisions, so he doesn't have a history of screwing up yet, and all of his needs and desires are fulfilled almost immediately: wet to dry, empty to full, edgy to relaxed, rocked asleep and then awake. You'd almost want to be Jax, if you didn't know what he was in store for — namely, a fully flawed human life. Stubbed toes, seventh grade, acne, broken hearts.

Sam can see now what beauty *he* sprang from, and how pathetically I loved him as a baby. It's unimaginable that we were all so perfect and lovely once, as opposed to our current conditions — awful, slightly scaly, plumping up, and in decay. Beckett said we were all bonny once. And babies' needs are achievable for the time being. They know they want something in their tummies; there's a lot of pleasure for them in fullness, in contact with warm skin, in the sweet circuit with the mother and father.

Jax is puzzled in a mellow, curious way, like "Huh? Now what? Excuse me, people, now something big and hairy is licking my ear."

I pissed off Amy by waking him up in his car seat so my friend Judy could meet him. Judy is famous in these parts as Miss Kitty, the folksinger who performs at *all* your better little kids' parties. I was in Stepford Wife mode, mad at Amy for being hours later than when she'd said they'd get here. Judy was ecstatic to meet Jax, and I think relieved that it was my son who was the father and not hers. We raised our boys together from when they were three, and we still hang out together. When Jax woke, he gaped at Judy like he knew she was a huge star in these parts, Beyoncé to the nursery set.

Jax was lovely and dear for a long time today, just delicious smells and wonder, and then sleepy, cranky, gritching, flapping and kicking, and then dropping off in my arms. But if I tried to shift my arm even an inch, he'd blink wide-awake — there's something so horror-movie about the way babies' eyes pop open, to *catch* you, like you're trying to escape. You feel like Daffy Duck when he finally gets away from the huge bad guy, and nails the door shut, but turns around to find the guy behind him in the same room.

Amy took a long bath here, and then painted my toenails even though I was mad at her for being late, and then for being mad at me, for being mad at her for being late. Aye-yi-yi. I was trying to suppress it but felt tense and sort of nuts. So it was definitely grace when she gave me a pedicure, with red toenail polish; it was a laying on of hands, like she used to do for Gertrud. Not that there is *any* correlation, I'm sure, between the way she intuitively knew how to care for that sometimes fussy old German woman, and youthful, adorable, endlessly patient me. . . .

Later Amy nursed, and when I put Jax, who was asleep, on the couch to change him, my dog Lily cleaned his ears. Then she got up in her usual space at the far end of the couch, by Jax's head. Her tail was slapping the couch like a windshield wiper, an inch from his face, and with each slap, I was trying to protect Jax's head from getting whapped, and miraculously Amy and I were in hysterics; slap slap slap. Jax slept, totally unaware that he was about to get a heavy, bushy tail right in the chops. I will start to take him to Judy's weekly sing-along for little kids, at Fort Baker, near the Golden Gate Bridge, as soon as he develops neck control. Miss Kitty makes up for a lot. Ask any kid in this county — they all grew up on her albums and performances. She had a boy in one music class who said, while listening to a concerto for oboe, "I *love* the hobo." And the little girl beside him said, "The hobo *rocks.*"

August 18
No further comments about Amy and Jax going to Chicago, although I know she wants to go soon. She is missing everyone

there terribly, and everyone is desperate to see her and the baby. Her grandmother is slipping away, and the estate pays for Amy to visit as often as possible. Trudy is there frequently, and will make a point of being there whenever Amy and Jax can visit, too.

My dear friend Neshama came for dinner, as she does most Tuesdays, even when there are other friends and family visiting. She loves my family, and they love her. I have been close to her since 1974, thirty-five years. She is in her seventies, with short gray fuzzy hair, reads as much as I, works at the Fairfax Library, and has three grandchildren who live in the East Bay, with whom she is close. I can tell her anything, even my ugliest thoughts. I confessed today that I love having a grandson partly because if Sam dies, which I've dreaded since *my* pregnancy test came back positive, then there will still be a mini-Sam. I asked her if she would hear my confession. Afterward, she said, "Oh, we all have it. It's genetics. It's what they call in England an heir and a spare." You need to have a lot of kids, because some of them will be killed by snakes and Visigoths. Plus you need to be sure someone will be there to change you when you're old.

On bad days, when life felt ludicrous, or

like we're all here in a big penal colony, my hilariously crabby Vedanta friend Karen used to look at her twin babies and think, What did you do last round to get sentenced to this joint? Arson?

August 21
This morning I called Sam to say hello, and it turned out that he and Amy had had a terrible argument the night before. She'd threatened again to take the baby to Chicago or go live with her parents in North Carolina. They'd had a long-drawn-out fight while window-shopping at Saks, and she'd left with Jax, just disappeared. So Sam, four months after quitting smoking, went straight into a smoke shop and bought a cigar (he didn't want to start smoking cigarettes again); he stepped outside, sat down on the curb, and started smoking it. He was apoplectic. He said that he started praying for a cougar — the human, female kind, i.e., a stunning and successful older woman — to come along and spoil him for the day. Or an Eskimo, like in the story I've told him since childhood, where the man crashes his plane in the tundra, then wakes up in a hospital, furious with God for not having been there to save him — He would have left him to die if this stupid Eskimo hadn't

finally come along.

But instead of Michelle Pfeiffer or Demi Moore, along came two middle-aged, heavily bearded East Indian men, one in a saffron robe. They walked past him, then backtracked. The man in the robe pointed to the cigar and said, with a heavy Indian accent, "The smoke is on the outside, but the problem is on the inside."

Sam said he felt as if he'd just been Tasered, but in a good way — a God shot. He thought, Are these guys my Eskimo?

He said, "You have my attention."

"Come with us and meditate," said the sidekick, also with a thick accent. "It will be what you need."

"How much will it cost?" Sam was hoping for a reason not to go.

The two men erupted in laughter. "What kind of meditating do *you* do? It costs nothing. Come with us."

Sam looked inward and wondered whether these guys had anything to do with his prayer for a cougar five minutes before, whether maybe God had gotten His signals crossed, but he decided to trust his gut that this is what God had sent in place of that.

He stood up and began walking with the cigar in his hand. One of the men said, with great authority, "You don't need that," so

Sam threw it onto Geary. The other man said, "No, no, someone needs that, just not you." So Sam retrieved it and put it on the curb. They went together down the street, to the apartment of a very kind woman whom Sam guessed was about forty, who has a small gathering every week. A group of eight people of all stripes were doing a standing meditation, moving slowly from foot to foot, chanting a mantra. He watched until they were done, and then ate a fresh vegetarian meal with them and talked about meditation. It turned out they met more formally on Sundays at a meditation center in beautiful Los Altos Hills, forty-five minutes southeast of the city, and they invited him to meet them there whenever he could make it. One of the men would teach him meditation, one of the women would teach Amy, and everyone would help mind Jax.

When Sam got home, he was so refreshed that it didn't really matter if Amy was still mad or not.

"Oh, no," I exclaimed over the phone in my most understanding way. "What if you become a Hare Krishna?"

"I'm not going to leave St. Andrew," he said. "But now me and Amy have free meditation teachers. Want to come to the ashram with the three of us on Sunday?"

I laughed and said I was teaching Sunday school.

"Well," he said. "I just knew you'd love this story. It's so you."

August 29

It is Sam's twentieth birthday today. Thank God; it sounds so much older. Another way of looking at it is that he is in his third decade now, so it doesn't seem like such a big deal that already he's a father. Yesterday it did, when he was nineteen.

He, Amy, and Jax went to the ashram in Los Altos Hills for the second Sunday in a row, for what is called kirtan — chanting, meditating, a vegetarian meal together afterward, with ten or so Indian and other Asian people. Dada, the man in the saffron robe, is the teacher of the people who gather on Sundays. He is visiting from India and is Sam's meditation teacher. Didi is Japanese and teaches the women, but she wasn't there that day. The universal mantra of the group is *Baba nam kevalam,* and I cannot get it out of my head. It is the most user-friendly mantra I have heard. It means: Love is all there is; everything is made of love, and love is who you are, period. Amy was offered rice, salad, dal, green olives, and two

64

fruit smoothies, one with honeydew and one with berries. But first she had to nurse Jax. Ragu, the other of the two men who had approached Sam on Geary, came over to sit with her in the living room while she finished nursing Jax, who then passed out. Ragu held him for half an hour while Amy and Sam ate with the other people in the kitchen and, as Amy reports, Dada was on the computer, doing only God knows what. Day trading? Facebook?

I feel so happy and hopeful that Sam and Amy have been given this tool. A miracle, and one I wish I had had. All of me is happy and relieved for Sam and Amy. You want your kids to have every break that might make life even slightly easier, because you know that no matter what, there are going to be very hard times. Yet sometimes I notice a swirl of jealousy in me, like a ribbon of caramel marbled into vanilla ice cream, that they have much more than I did when Sam was an infant. They have three parents who have done all right in the world, who have disposable income. They sometimes seem to take this for granted, if you ask my tiny personal self. They both have good cars, Amy an SUV she inherited from her grandparents, with only fifty thousand miles on it, and Sam a great six-year-old truck with a minuscule cab that I helped him buy for his eighteenth birthday. I had such a rattletrap car when he was born, my mother's battered two-door Corolla, which I called the Joadmobile. Of course, I also had fantastically generous friends, as well as St. Andrew and other fellowships where I could take Sam. And I did meditate, in my frenetic and worried way, "*Om mane padme hum,* I wonder if the baby is breathing, *Om mane padme hum,* I hate that guy's moustache at church, *Om mane padme hum,* my butt itches, I wonder if it is cancer."

Twenty years ago, against many odds — age, being alone, scarcity — I got to have the one thing I wanted more than anything else on earth, a child. It was hard, and it is still hard, and it shall be hard all the days of our lives.

September 11

Sam called to say that he and Amy have been fighting and she has a one-way ticket to North Carolina to live with her parents. This is his version, at least.

I am experiencing sickening fear, the need to control, and the ubiquitous litany of good ideas. I thank God again and again that my mind does not have a public address system

66

or an open mike every evening.

I guess Amy's leaving is predictable — to expect them to keep it together in a tiny apartment was unrealistic. Babies are hard enough for couples in love who have college degrees, and homes, and help. But this way is wrenching.

I was so miserable after talking to Sam that I had to call horrible Bonnie, my mentor. She was no help at all. She said that Amy would go to North Carolina to find out what she needed to know — namely, what it will be like to live with her parents as an adult, and how long she can be away from Sam, me, St. Andrew, our life here.

Bonnie pointed out that all three of them are kids, in what feels like an untenable situation. Sam and Amy don't have big coping skills yet. And, Bonnie added, "they don't actually even have fully developed cerebral cortexes yet." They are ground down constantly by the pressures of their lives, exhaustion, and the needs of this little baby.

For Sam there will be grief, and a measure of relief, because of the demands of school, and that he'll feel guilty about.

The situation is so Amy — the same impetuous, fiery, hardheaded quality that is also the miraculous force that created Jax, insisted on having him, and worked through the heroic labor.

Bonnie persuaded me to focus on the good, just for today: tomorrow I can call back and we will wallow in the total awfulness of Amy's behavior, which will surely lead to permanent estrangement and dead bodies. Just for today, I was supposed to try to remember three things:

The baby is not falling off the earth, or headed to Afghanistan.

So many things are going well: Everyone has good health. Jax is perfect.

Even though I have acid and sewage and grippage in my stomach, which I have had many times before and will have many times again, I can build faith muscles by bearing my feelings of misery and powerlessness — a kind of Nautilus. Rumi said that through love, all pain would turn to medicine. But he never met my family. Or me.

I took the one action I could think of, besides calling Bonnie and praying. I wrote Amy's name down on a bit of paper and put it in my god box, an old Sunshine Biscuits tin that I use as a mail drop to God. "Here," I said to Jesus, with enormous hostility, "have a go at it," and closed the lid.

Inwardly I believe that by this grippage, this not letting go, I am holding people safe, although a critic might point out that I am holding them in a death grip. It doesn't help them to stay safe! It doesn't let them move around. Or learn their lessons. Or grow up. So there's that. Fine. I am impeding the flow of spirit for everyone else, and creating psychic indigestion for me. God, it's awful to see what crap we have inside us. It all feels too hard right now, certainly for Amy.

She won't know that she has to move through her discomfort, not escape from it, until she flees. To me it feels heedless and cruel. She sees it as steeliness, not meanness or panic. She needs more help than Sam gives her.

I called Bonnie again — statistically, it has been proven nine times out of ten that *simply* talking to a trusted person helps in most tough situations. Saying my problems out loud is the main way I am ever able to let go. People say in chipper voices, "Let go and let God," and I think, "Oh, fuck you."

Now I can't remember for sure if that has been proven statistically.

Bonnie said that Amy has to do what she has to do; that I can't control, absorb, fix, or change her inside process. I *hate* that, I told Bonnie, and said I wouldn't call her anymore.

"Good night, dearest," Bonnie said, laughing. "You know, I'm up reading for at least another hour if you need me."

September 12

I woke up in extreme mental distress. It was barely six; I must have been flopping around, because Lily was standing over me, peering down from a few inches away, to see if I was even alive after my fall to the canyon floor.

The only person I know who is awake this early is Neshama, so I called her. After filling her in on the latest, I said, "I have a splitting headache, and what if Amy really moves for good, and I hardly ever see Jax again? Motherhood trumps everything — the courts will decide in her favor. . . ."

"Wait," Neshama said nicely. "Which courts are we talking about?"

I sighed and managed a quiet laugh. She said in the course of our talk that I was remarkable, having used all possible spiritual tools, of breath, prayer, putting it all on a note in the god box, and, as now, the thousand-pound phone. (Why is it so hard to pick up the phone and reach out for help? My arm muscles tremble as I lift it, like it's a shot put.)

"Plus your animals are solace and won't flee."

"The dogs have gone back to sleep. Fat lot of good they do me."

"They just feel useless in the face of your tears. They have no hands, or pockets for their money and ID. Besides, crying is good — it's a steam spigot, pressure relief, but you have to turn it off so you don't move into — heaven forbid! — bathos. So dogs, breath, prayer, phone, crying, god box, aspirin, and chocolate as needed. And call me in the afternoon."

September 13

I had been commemorating Mitts off the Kids Day, not calling either of them to nudge, pry, prey. Instead I was trying to release them to the care of their higher powers, to trust that everyone's greatest good was always being revealed, even if it was a nightmare for me until then. This was going poorly, until we had an apocalyptic lightning storm — fantastic, like the first moments of Earth — and Amy called so we could ooh and aah at the same time. That crashing explosion brought us together. She reported that Jax was sleeping through it in Sam's arms. He didn't even twitch at the thunder, safe in Sam's warmth. And there was a small upturn — wait, wait, make that a great and major improvement. Amy and Jax are still leaving, but now they have a round-trip ticket, and will be back in about three weeks. Thank you, Jesus, thank you thank you thank you. Will never doubt You again, et cetera, this is the new me.

A friend of Tom's says that grace is a small white butterfly, and life is a semi trailer careening up 101.

September 17

I called Bonnie to check in, and tell her that Jax and Amy were gone, and how high my psychic viral load was. I have these morbid, terrifying fantasies — but I had the same ones before Jax was born, that the baby would die and Sam would commit suicide. It's the wild horses ready to tear apart the whole world.

But you created these horses, Bonnie pointed out. Then you tied them to the trees and gave them a flick on the butt. They're figment horses, false-evidence-appearing-real horses. If you don't tie the horses up, they just racket around, and that's not so bad, because they burn up the wild energy. So don't tie up the anxiety fantasies, either.

Bonnie asked, "Just for today, would you be willing to look at all the goodness that is present as a result of this mess?"

Okay, fine. The most important thing is

that everyone is about to get more knowledge, that he or she will then be able to use — Amy, Sam, Nana.

But I told Bonnie I could not bear the pain that Sam was in, and would face the next few weeks. She wondered if I didn't think I could bear my *own* pain. She said that Sam was strong, spiritual, and very, very busy. So, I asked, the good part of my pain would be . . . ? She said, "You've got to learn to let go and let your children fall, and fail. If you try to protect them from hurt, and always rush to their side with Band-Aids, they won't learn about life, and what is true, what works, what helps, and what are real consequences of certain kinds of behavior. When they do get hurt, which they will, they won't know how to take care of their grown selves. They won't even know where the aspirin is kept."

She apparently thinks the good part is that God has such huge, great love for them, whereas I think it is unaddressably bad news that they will get so badly hurt in life.

One thing I figured out for myself is that Jax's life, parents, grandparents, and teeny fragile body are a clumsy, messy container for the very precious soul, as is true for all of us. Jax needs a mother who doesn't feel she is going to flip out. So it's great that

Amy got in touch with what she needed to do for her own mental health.

The miracle for me would be to go from clench and sick stomach, to release and a little bit of faith. Unfortunately, I do not want the miracle. I want Jax, and Jax is gone.

September 22, Interview with Sam
"How are you doing, Little Bear?"

There's a silence, a bad silence. "Mom? I'm twenty, I have a child. Do you think it might be possible for you to stop calling me Little Bear?"

Garbled death noise from Annie, stabbed-through-heart noises, mortification.

"Mom? Are you there? Could you just not call me Little Bear *today?*"

Another garbled sound of self-loathing; also, maybe throat cancer.

Sigh: "Mom, it's really okay. I'm really rushed, I have a project due. Okay, in answer to your question: Half of me feels devastated, screwed over, fucked up. Sometimes I ache, like when I was in withdrawal from cigarettes; and I hurt every time I think about him, and your legs start going crazy, like you might have to run for a long time just so you won't lose it. But then you have to tell your body to relax, and get back to homework. I have a gigantic workload, and without Jax I actually have about ten extra hours a day. So to be honest, I'm not so judgmental about men who run off. I used to think, 'How could anyone *ever* leave their baby or child? Just take off and pretend it never happened?' I would never, ever run — I've made my decision. But I get it now. I've got an empty house, it's nice and quiet, or I get to play loud music at all hours, and get to have friends over whenever I want. I remember what freedom feels like. And I saw the appeal of running."

September 25, Interview with Sam
"Sam, in what way are you like me as a parent that you are glad about?"

"Oh, that's hugely easy. I'm glad I'm hard-working like you, and that I naturally love to play with my kid, and that I'm sort of flexible for such a rigid, uptight guy. I'll eventually go with whatever might just work.

"What Jax will thank you for giving me is my ability to forgive and start over. Not everyone has it, and I can't believe I do. I'm glad for two reasons. One, that I can do it, even though it's hard, because you're doomed if you can't, and two, when you can do it, you start finding people in the world like you, who can start over, too, and these are the people you want to be with.

People who can forgive.

"It's so incredibly humbling when someone forgives you — I can't ever believe when people forgive me, because you know how badly you've screwed up, and how you've hurt them, and how hard it is for them to be brave enough to find it in themselves to reexperience the pain *you* caused, and the humiliation that is in them because of you — and for someone to be willing to refeel that much like shit again, reexperience it out of not wanting to lose you, means how deeply precious you are to them. And that's pure gold."

"And in what ways are you like me as a parent that you hate?"

"The worrying. I swore I'd never be like you, have the obsessive psycho worry about my kid. But I can put Jax in his stroller, he's totally safe, warm, with protective me beside him, and I go to put my socks on, and instantly I imagine his face too close to his Mr. Bear blanket, and think of how you're not supposed to put anything plush or fluffy near babies' mouths and noses — it's an instant death sentence, because fluffy things capture the CO_2, and the baby suffocates in that — and I can see that the blanket is only *inches* away from his face, and I have to pull it down because otherwise it's a lethal object, full of death air, like when a kidnapper holds a rag of chloroform over your face to knock you unconscious. But here it's only a fleecy blanket someone made for us, with a cute little silky bear head in the corner."

September 27
I organized a field trip to the ashram in Los Altos with Sam and Neshama, partly to share the experience with Sam, partly because I knew it would help him stay strong; it's also maybe a tiny unattractive moment of revenge against Amy. She has already been gone for well over a week, and won't be back for a week and a half or so. Sam told me on the way down, "What tipped me off the first night on Geary that Dada and Ragu were not going to kill me was that there were all these people, repeating in Sanskrit that love is all there is, love is all there is, *Baba nam kevalam.* Plus, there was no charge." That's my boy.

The ashram was a house with one large bedroom set up as a place of worship. Neshama and I felt at home instantly. The community of nine was so welcoming, many of the same people who were at the apartment where Sam went the night he had first met Dada and Ragu. Dada had gone to the orphanage that he and Ragu run in India. Ragu is the uncle who has summoned us all, young and old Indian people, other Asians, a few whites. He is the common thread. He's stocky, ample, very vigorous and composed at the same time. His skin has a purple-brown twinkle, like an eggplant. He's furry and he looks like a gypsy, the embodiment of the whole morning, which was also vigorous and composed.

The room was wonderfully modest, an off-white bedroom in a house way out in the hills. The thick caramel-colored carpet muffles the sound. There are beautiful plastic orchids on the altar — just a reminder of true flowers, but without a fortune spent on the trappings. Same with the cheap lace on the altar; it says: This place of worship is so beautiful that we don't need to spend a lot of energy and money on saying that. People don't need to lose their eyesight embroidering cloths that will degrade. Store your treasures in heaven, and all that. Chant with us, be with us, help make the meal.

The service began with a man playing tabla, and an old Jewish-looking Indian man on harmonium: such a strange sound! If we could breathe loudly, this is the sound our lungs would make. It's elegant and portable;

he pumped and noodled it without virtuosity; he's humble and lovely, just letting his fingers play, because they know what to do, without ego or performance. Neshama said later that it's a community instrument — he's the fingers playing it for all of us, he provides breathing and rest, while the drumbeat gives us the impetus to motion.

We danced, first taking slow baby steps and then upping the ante, going faster and faster to the blasting stomp; and then starting over, slowly, without exhausting ourselves, but still with the feeling of going through detox, breaking down pockets of stored toxins and expelling them through tribal stomp. It was gloriously ridiculous — Sam told me before we came that at first it's as embarrassing as doing karaoke, but then he forgets about himself: which would be my definition of heaven. He was in front of me, dancing with such dignity I could have cried.

We all sat down to meditate, and even though I thought mostly about the food that was going bad in my fridge that I'd meant to throw out, and my achy knee, sitting amid all that was positive calmed me way down.

Ragu is what you'd like in a parent — he nudges you to participate. He encourages you with his devout twinkles, and he's very safe — welcoming and grounded. He doesn't lean on you and breathe on you the way your parents would; he lets you come to it. Lots of encouragement, with no hot breath. Note to self: Start being more like Ragu.

For once, I was not noisy niggles and snickets, in all that internal and external chaos and noise and thought; I just relaxed into the moment, and fell into the sweetness of the universe, as if I were snorkeling.

An older father held his baby, who was quiet and good during the meditation, as though taking it in directly, sensing he was in an absolutely marvelous space, with the chanting and the rhythms when his parents held him in their arms for the sacred dance. Or maybe they had dosed him with baby Tylenol, as I would have done.

When we got to our feet to do *Baba nam,* I watched Sam, his eyes closed and arms extended like Zorba in dancing prayer, shifting from foot to foot, and this filled me with respect for his ability to let go, to go within himself and find a center. I did not have this at twenty, not by a long shot.

We did this for half an hour, shifting, chanting, *Baba nam kevalam.* Watching Sam in worship, welcomed and respected by these great people, I was deeply touched at how much he has grown, as I am sometimes when I watch him casually change a seriously bad diaper on my couch. Sam talked with people easily over our simple lunch of rice and curried vegetables, and salad with nuts and green olives. Later, Ragu gave us apples from the ashram's trees to take home, and everyone crowded around us, but most of them suddenly wanted our e-mail addresses, and I thought, "Oh, *no*. Now I'll *never* get rid of these people."

October 1

Sam came by for dinner and to do homework at my big table. He hasn't heard much from Amy, and I didn't pry — much. Trying to be like Ragu has not been going quite as well as I had hoped, but I managed to offer Sam a little more silence than I have in months. Silence brings you to a place where all of a sudden you're not in the mental ping-pong game. I made us an organic cornmeal pizza, and read while I ate; he was watching a whaling show out of the corner of his eye on TV, while drawing something on his sketch pad for class, and I let him be, although of course I was having tiny thoughts about good study habits. Sometimes you can see around the edges of what's right before you, instead of what you are fixated on, specifically how Sam is doing with Amy and Jax gone. Message to self: Step *back*, because then you can pick up stuff that is actually going right. He was working on a drawing of a 3-D pyramid, which I bent in to admire. This pleased him, and helped me abide his sadness without needing to fix it; and so I saw the beauty of his contemplation. Maybe what we say to each other is not so important after all, but just that we are alive together, and present for each other as best as we can be.

October 3

Sam called and woke me up late tonight, to say he will not be in church, as he has a ton of homework, plus he needs to clean the house before Amy and Jax get home. I couldn't get back to sleep; I was too keyed up thinking about seeing Jax again, but even more energized about Sam's getting to see Jax. This is sort of pathetic.

Sam seems reasonably grounded — overwhelmed, and excited, and worried. I was truly desperate with fretfulness and guilty ambition at his age, although I looked happy and accomplished. There are so many things I did right as a parent: times we spent playing and building with Legos and blocks on the floor; all those card games at the kitchen table; creating a relatively low-stress home, without a man with whom to quibble about arrangements, money, and whether we were having sex enough. I was derailed from the cradle by the stress of my parents' unhappy marriage. I had no self-esteem during my youth, no matter how much I achieved. This is common for children who were raised by wolves. It was like the parents were *trying* to be terrible. Or were punking you. You realize at some point that your parents did their best and that this should lead to forgiveness. For me, it led to awe. Bad awe. It was part of the global realization that the adult world was about falsehood, appearance, mediocrity, and precarious mental states.

I said to Sam before we hung up, "I know you haven't seen him in a couple of weeks, but what is the difference now in how you experience Jax?" He replied, "When he first came to us, he was a little lump of a guy, and we were very tired. I felt like I'd known him for a while. Now he's a person, and I can't remember not knowing him."

October 4

I went to church crankily because it is stewardship month, and I hate the shakedown sermons, but I had to go because I was teaching Sunday school. Also, Sam wouldn't be there, or Ragu, or the harmonium guy. I was comparing St. Andrew with the ashram, and coming up short, like we were tense southern snake-handler types.

Is it really true that everyone, including me, is growing and healing spiritually, whether we experience that or not? It sure didn't feel that way. Bonnie and Tom both think so, although they point out that growth is not fast, clean, cute, or comfortable. It would be great if God were up there shoving ever-resistant people like me through the maze, toward presence and serenity. But noooo. It's Free Will 101. This does not work for me at all. Still, I went to church — bitterly — because of the Sunday-school kids.

Only there *were* no kids, except in the nursery. I hung out with Jax's colleagues, Isaiah and Cooper, and their teacher, until Jax's absence began to feel like a cavern. I came; I pined; I headed back to church for the stewardship sermon.

And everyone there conspired to ruin my best efforts to wallow in self-pity. The four oldest women with their walkers, wheelchairs, and wigs in the Amen corner snagged me first. Billie Johnson's hair looked especially pretty, and when I commented on this she said, "Oh, I just found this old one in the hamper." She made me hug and kiss her for so long that I remembered Sam at age five, unable to part with me one night, heartbroken that I was going out; he said, like a sad old man, "Let me keep kissing you until I can stop crying." The gentle, tough, crying, laughing, singing congregation is such an unfair advantage on God's part; it really sucks. Then Ranola sang the lead in the choir anthem, and her voice was as peaceful as the pristine silence of the ashram — it's just the other side of it, of what carves out space, so we can rest into what's bigger than us. Her voice, the choir, the quietness at the ashram, are paradoxically like burrowing into the snow to make a shelter that covers and surrounds tiny you and keeps you warm.

I girded myself against Veronica and her stewardship sermon, and then she preached one of her best sermons ever. She began by talking about the German word for "sin," which she said means "to separate, to sunder" — so that instead of seeing our divine nature, we see our separation everywhere, from one another, from God, from our own souls. It reminded me of a line I've had taped to my wall for years: "We aren't a drop in the ocean, but are the ocean, in drops."

Veronica said that no matter how painful and wrong things seem, Jesus is always playing the music softly in our lives, and we can dance around, because when we dance with one another, everyone feels happier, and chosen, and we are dancing with the godhead, of which we are a part. Then she made us get up and dance around.

I am not making this up.

All forty of us danced — Evelyn in her wheelchair, Marge Cortez with her cane. A sleeping baby was danced in his mother's arms; and the rest of us held hands or hips in a conga line, or did the foxtrot, or, like me, the Bolinas hippie tribal stomp. Ike danced with his oxygen tank.

I went home and danced around as I cleaned the house, too happy to contain myself, because on top of it all, coincidentally, ha ha, almost three weeks had miraculously passed somehow, and Jax would be home tomorrow.

October 6

I didn't know what the mood would be like when the three of them came over for the first time again, late this afternoon. When they came, Sam and Amy were not getting along; Sam was being a poophead, nagging, napping, and then going out to use his cell phone, and Amy was frustrated and stuck with Jax, who lay on the couch in his perfection and slept, while I watched a little TV with her and made snacks. Then I sat on the porch with Sam and laughed a little about what morons the dogs are, and went to my study and got a little bit of work done while Amy watched judge shows, and then we had grilled cheese and tomato sandwiches, with baby carrots and slices of autumn apples. Against all odds, it was kind of okay, with friendly moments of conversation around the TV, about the baby, the news, the filling and delicious food. We laughed a number of times, and having come out of a tense, miserable place earlier, I found a surprising peace in that. This family business can be so stressful — difficult, damaged people showing up to spend time with other difficult, damaged people, time that might be better used elsewhere — yet out of that, some accidental closeness, laughter, some pieced-together joy.

October 12, Interview with Sam
"Sam, what are the main differences you see in Jax, and yourself, after weeks of not seeing each other?"

"Before he left, when it was milk time, that was it. He'd be buried in the boob, obsessed. Now, if something even slightly interesting happens, he'll look up, detach from the nipple, see what it is.

"When I come along, he'll look up like he's a businessman, and this is not a good time for him — can we talk later?

"And he's crazily more vocal. More basic vowel sounds. He's convinced he's communicating with us. His understanding is that there is no real organization to speaking — there's nothing to it! You just call stuff out and then the other person just randomly squawks back at you.

"We're on different time and years. I have to orbit a much bigger planet, so time is slow, but Jax's planet is tiny, and he makes a complete orbit in a few hours. In one hour he can go from no coordination with, say, his pinkie, and in a couple of hours, he has the beginnings of control — or at least the concept of what control of his pinkie might be.

"When he watches me and Amy dance around the room, he registers how complexly we are moving. We put on music because it's good for him, to let him see the complexity of motion and also us being close and happy — and we think he knows how simple he is compared to us. But when he dances with us, he gets a direct connection to that complexity. He strives for what he sees us doing.

"I think he understands that he is not like us yet — that he still needs to be cared for, that he can't just walk around. But also, he knows he is evolving every day. Watching us dance, I think he's thinking, 'Wow, that looks cool. I would like to do that. Maybe we learn that next week.'

"One day I'll be playing with his arms and dangling stuff in front of him to try and get him to grab it — and by the end of that session, he'll have come a tiny ways, and then the next day he slowly starts from where he finally got to the day before, the slow reaching.

"Before, his arms were tight and tucked in, and I would unfold them so he could have the experience of length. Or I would encourage him to unfold his arms, but before, he could only grab his face.

"But now he can freely reach for nothing."

October 20
Amy and I celebrated Jax's three-month birthday today with a feast of rice and beans, with lime-juice bars for dessert. Jax

is a good baby. He almost never cries, just looks around, and into our faces, and makes his funny baby sounds. I said to Amy, "We have all loved your son's time on earth with us so far, and want only continued health, growth, and comfort. However, rules are rules, and at this time we are required to review what he has learned so far in his first three months."

She looked at me like I was nuts, then got out a notebook as if she were my secretary.

I said that he had successfully mastered an understanding of the basic concepts, transitioning from distress and uncomfortable states to relief and temporary improvement. From hungry to full, cold to warm, wet to dry, anxiety to breast, bored to watching funny people. I said he got an A+, which she put at the top of her paper, and circled.

We listened together for a while to his sounds, coos and peeps and snorfles. Listening to him is my single favorite thing about life these days, along with holding him in my arms while he sleeps. Not long ago, I told my friend Leo how bad my back has been lately, and he said he has a guy in Minneapolis who could help me, a master Chinese orthopedic surgeon who now heals people by doing *tui na*, Chinese bodywork massage with acupuncture, while making what sound like soft bird and pig imitations. Leo said I would have to step out on my faith, though, because the man is brilliant but not board-certified; he hasn't been able to take the boards in the United States because his *English* sounds like bird and pig imitations, too.

Maybe *he* would know what Jax is trying to say.

October 30, Interview with Sam
"How are you doing, darling?"

"Bummed. Bad. I can't find any balance now between school, and Amy and Jax. I can't schedule any Sam time, not any at all, just to sit with myself. My classes are kicking my butt. The Core classes you have to pour yourself into, because if you do great models, it goes into your portfolio. The rest are stepping-stone classes, in the sense that they are prerequisites to the Core classes, but I think I need to take more of them because I can't manage the extreme time pressure of the one Core class you are expected to take each term. Every teacher so far has been great, though, so I guess I just have to figure out a way to calm myself and be grateful, instead of being a jerk. But I'm not there yet. I'm disappointed with myself, not being able to do more. I'm barely hanging on. It's going to take me five years to graduate instead of four, which is frustrating. It makes me feel like kind of a loser, because I want to get on with my life, and not be in school. I'd like to be working full-time, and take care of my son. Best case would be to work for myself. Worst case would be on a salary, because after you have a kid, money suddenly seems like such a stupid thing to work for all your life. But all of this is the price of having Jax. I'm kind of okay with it. I mean, what are my choices?"

"Are things different between you and God, since you had Jax?"

"Well, when I'm talking to God, it's still Him and me, which I love, because with friends and family, it all ultimately ends up being about Jax. With God, I don't feel pressured to talk about Jax. I guess with Jax, I feel more like a brother than a dad, because we're so close in age. I feel kind of like a taxi driver trying to get God from place to place. I sure don't feel like a TV dad. It's more like being in God's Secret Service: my job is to protect this kid and his destiny.

"I feel desperate of him — maybe that's not correct grammatically, but I feel *desperate* of him.

"I had no idea how damaged I was until I

had a kid — how totally powerless. I feel about him like you do when you hold a really young, vulnerable baby kitten that's not quite at the age when you're supposed to pick it up. Like, if he chooses not to smile at me, or is fixated on Amy, I feel just crushed. Or when we're hanging out with Kenny Boo's kid Amari, I totally realize how crazy I am, because Amari is two months older, and I know that, but I still compare him and Jax. Jax isn't nearly as tough as Amari — he might even be *afraid* of Amari. Then I feel so self-conscious — of *Jax.* Because he's so little and inept! He has all these tics, and spazzy moves, as if I have this shrimpy little Tourette's person, but Amari is mellow and cool, like George Clooney. I know at five months old, which is how old Amari is, you get quieter because your nerves are better and you're much more together. But still! I worry that Jax's hands aren't big enough — I mean, Amari's are baseball mitts compared to his. God, can you even believe this? The cross we bear is self-consciousness. But Jax is really a perfect baby. I'm sickeningly in love with him."

"What can Jax do now that he couldn't do before?"

"Oh my God. He can bring his *foot* to his

mouth. I mean, YO. I bet you can't do that anymore. I call it his foot phone. I say, Jax is on the foot phone now. Alex Babakitis and I used to do this when we were about ten. We'd put one of our feet by one of our ears, and talk to our foot. We'd say, 'Hello? Oh, sorry, wrong number,' and then hang up our foot.

"He's reaching for more and more. If he has a goal, like the plastic rings on his car seat, and tries for them, but it doesn't go well, he stops and wriggles his hands back and forth. Sometimes he can do it perfectly — get what he reaches for — other times it doesn't go so smoothly, and then he Etch A Sketches it — shakes his hands up to start over.

"It's all changing. It's getting more real."

November 1

The Day of the Dead is today and tomorrow, so I invited Millard, Stevo, Jax's cousin Clara, Sam, Jax, Amy, and cousin Neshama for a party; Annette had to work. It's such a great holiday, so we can remember life by celebrating food and colors as the days grow darker and colder, smokier; it's a time of deep change. We're moving into the darkest time of the year. I have a huge beautiful photo on my dining room wall, of an older woman selling marigolds from a wheel-barrow on the Day of the Dead in Mexico. She looks like a jack-o'-lantern, with her broad face and enormous teeth. She's rooted and grounded and solid, but she's also aloft with joy. Her wheelbarrow holds hundreds of flowers in a tumble, all held together somehow, yet at the same time exuberantly spilling over.

Sam and Amy seemed really close today, and Sam was especially glad to be with Millard, who has lost even more weight, so he actually looks like a Day of the Dead figurine. I had decorated the house and lit the darkness with bright flowers and candles, and everyone shuffled in through the piles of dead leaves outside, hunched over in heavier clothes. Clara alone stopped to jump in the leaves, wearing an embroidered blouse that I got her in Mexico. She has come through the bad divorce between her mother and Stevo with her spirit more than intact. She is blonde and funny, really the light of our lives. She bent her knees to jump. You can't jump until you sink down a little. And when you are aloft, there is always such dark and sad stuff underneath, below you. But if you touch down into it first, it helps you get aloft.

November 3

Jax and Amy were here all day. Jax can now scrunch up his face into what Sam calls his Hard Look, with his brow furrowed, while he splutters and drools. It is just terrifying. What next? Will he start giving me the finger?

I think about the idea of his having dual citizenship — a child of God and heaven, with a human life here — and how confusing that has always been for me. And what he is in for, because our spiritual and human identities coexist, the way light is both a particle and a wave.

November 4

I bought a ticket today to meet my friend Bill Hanson in Delhi around the time of Jax's six-month birthday. Now I cannot remember why that seemed like a good idea. The timing is dicey, because there's so much on my plate — Jax, Millard beginning to fail, the book I'm pretending to write — but I need something bigger to shake up my snow globe, and boy, this is bigger.

I'm stuck in the usual small neuroses and obsessive pain, but India is global dreams and madness. Is it crazy that I am going? Maybe deliciously ludicrous.

Bill has been to India many times, and

speaks a little Hindi, and always said he would meet me if I could get myself there. He never thought in a million years that I could do it. He's great; hardly anyone makes me laugh harder. The fact that I might have a nervous breakdown if I can't see Jax for two weeks: reason enough to go.

Plus I had hundreds of thousands of frequent-flyer miles from various book tours. Although that does not explain why something inside me picked the single hugest, most sprawling, grotesque place on earth. I guess the left brain doesn't know what the right brain is doing.

Usually, when I travel, I want to go only between the pages of a book — or a movie. So I'm going there in person, to compare, contrast, and gape. I want to see what I've been seeing my whole life in movies, the giddily colorful amid the squalor, right out there on the streets for all to see. A pantheon of wild deities who are everywhere, embodied in cows wandering in traffic, holy men, murals, cow dung, and storefront temples. The celebrations of death in the river that you also *bathe* in — all the elements present at the same time in these moments: earth, fire and ash, air, water, dung.

Is dung an element? It may as well be.

November 5, Interview with Sam

"Hello, darling. Tell me the latest."

"The main thing is that even when Jax was new, you could make plans, even though you knew the plans wouldn't work out. Before, I'd wake up at eight, walk to school, work ten hours, come home. Now I wake at six-thirty, help get the morning started, which takes forever, walk to school, work eight hours, be behind, *always* be behind.

"Two weeks ago, if Jax was fussy, you could bend down and smile, and he'd come right back to happy. Now the human quality of his not always being fine has come out — doors are opening for him. Now if you don't smile right or pick him up the exact way he likes, he makes his mad face at you — the Hard Look — and he might not get over it for a whole minute. He'll make unhappy, frustrated farting noises at you, and he has the face to go with it — doing this for about sixty seconds is his limit now, but I can see that, like you always say, it is *all* downhill from here. It's *all* over for England."

November 7

The mother of a boy Sam went to school with since first grade came up to me at the health food store today and asked if it was true. "Is it true?" she said, in full-tilt, fake-concerned schadenfreude. Her son, whom I adore, is in his sophomore year at Berkeley. When Jax first arrived, and parents of Sam's friends would either tell me how great it was or ask how things were going, I would lapse into an embarrassed explanation — I'd say that I'd always longed to be a grand-parent, but of course had thought it would be in another ten years or so, and I'd paw at the ground and repeat, "But who asked me?" This always got a laugh. Mostly every-one has been sweet and positive about Sam's having a baby, except for one mother who lives in our neighborhood, who has been very distant, as if we were a cautionary tale and contagious, or as if Sam had joined the Taliban. But today I showed the woman in the health food store my most recent pictures of one of the handsomest babies anyone has ever seen, and one of Sam hold-ing him, both of them looking like Gap models, and one of Amy, so beautiful, hold-ing out a laughing Jax toward the camera. And as the mother oohed and aahed, I thought to myself, This is the single greatest fucking thing that has ever happened to me.

November 9
The only son of some people Sam and I

99

know from town has died.

How on earth can the parents survive that? How can the grandparents?

Same old inadequate answer: They will survive with enormous sadness and devastation. I don't see how that is possible. But looking back over the years, I see that people do go on against absolutely all odds, and truly savage loss.

Some of us have a raggedy faith. You cry for a long time, and then after that are defeated and flattened for a long time. Then somehow life starts up again. Other people set up foundations so other kids don't die the way theirs did, and so their kids didn't die in vain, or they do political work for the common good. Your friends surround you like white blood cells. It's just fucking unbelievably sad, pretty much forever, when so much love and life have been packed into one person and then the person dies too soon. But you can shake your fist at the void with scorn and say, "You didn't get her, you bastard. We did." Some aching beauty comes with huge loss, although maybe not right away, when it would be helpful. Life is a very powerful force, despite the constant discouragement. So if you are a person with connections to life, a few tendrils eventually break through the sidewalk of loss, and you

100

notice them, maybe space out studying them for a few moments, or maybe they tickle you into movement and response, if only because you have to scratch your nose.

November 10, Sam by Phone
"I'm blown away by how beautiful Jax's skin is. He has brown legs, like Amy's. I do not. I have see-through legs. I got this from *you,* Mom. You don't realize how tan, what a rich color he has to him, until you see him lying next to me, like a baby Mayan, with a white radioactive daddy."

November 11
A friend of Amy's and mine blurted out this morning while we were walking the dogs on the ridge that Amy told her she is thinking of having Jax baptized at her old Catholic church in Chicago. The floor dropped out from under me, and I roared, "She's thinking of what?" Then the friend hemmed and hawed, and said, Well, a date's actually been set. Amy and her parents apparently planned it when she was with them in North Carolina.

I pooh-poohed the ridiculousness of this with a wave, and we continued walking along the ridge in the fog. Instantly I was in Richard Nixon levels of twitch and paranoia

and glower. I faked equanimity, which is my
strong suit, and pointed out the few autumn
wildflowers: buttercups and white milk-
maids. But betrayal and suspicion streaked
across my mind like vapor trails.

I felt so crazed that I had to call horrible
Bonnie, even though I knew she would say
that something beautiful was being revealed.
Luckily she wasn't home. I called Neshama,
who said wisely that Amy is desperate to
mark her space, to even have a space of her
own at all. She said I must seem like such a
threat, because I have such huge love for
and from Jax, while Amy wants to be the
font of love for him, the Vaillancourt Foun-
tain on the Embarcadero.

Yes, this was true. I'm the enforcer, the
matriarch, the bank. And Neshama said
Amy wants, like most mothers, for the
circuit to be her and Jax. Sam gets to be a
part of their circuit, but all mothers need to
protect their babies from their mothers-in-
law. I sighed, and told her that this oldest of
all jokes filled me with self-loathing.

"Well," said Neshama, "almost everything
does, at first. So you call your friends. Amy
may have some reason why she doesn't want
to release him to St. Andrew. Maybe she is
currying favor with her family, with her
grandmother and relatives who live in

Chicago. She identifies with being Catholic, even though she loves St. Andrew. Didn't you tell me she names her religion on Facebook as Catholicism?" I grudgingly admitted this was true. "Yet maybe," Neshama continued, "it's not that at all. Maybe she's simply groping in the dark for a place where she can make her stand."

My religious faith is based almost entirely on having brilliant, tenderhearted friends, and I had faith in life again when I hung up, aside from enormous sadness, anger, resentment, derision, and need for revenge. I have just enough wellness to know that the baptism is a symbolic act — it's not what will forge Jax's spiritual and religious character. And that for me to express my disapproval backs Amy into a corner, and sets up a negative interface with me.

I could call Amy and bring it up — bring it out of the closet — gently, by saying, "I was really hoping you would do it at the church where Sam and I were baptized, so our family could be there."

Nah.

The aikido move would be to get out of her way, and not confront her.

If I did, it would give us both space, and breathing room.

But I didn't want breathing space. I

wanted Jax baptized at St. Andrew.

Amy was saying, I'm a grown-up and I get to decide what's right for my son.

I didn't know if Sam knew yet. Maybe he was in on it, too. The two of them sat around thinking, "What would hurt Annie the most? I know! We could refuse to get Jax baptized at her church." Then they laughed demonically.

I hate to be the person whom people have to protect themselves from, as Sam had to do all those years, as all kids have to do to some degree.

I took the dogs for another walk. I couldn't give it up, convinced that I could steer it correctly, and help everyone see the absurdity of it, and game it this way, and veer away from that. It's like I think I'm so good at pinball — whereas the only victory is to walk away from the entire machine after one more defeat.

An obtrusive radical thought entered my mind: Jax is being baptized through his eyes and ears every time he comes to St. Andrew, by the people there, their love and warmth — to consecrate. Then another thought, even more radical: Amy's higher power is working through her, and with her, and I'm not it.

November 11

I called Bonnie at ten, and told her the story of the plans for the baptism, and when I was done, there was a silence, and I knew it was going to be bad.

After a moment, she said, "Annie? Isn't this really between Amy and Sam?"

That literally had not occurred to me.

Then Tom happened to call after I got off the phone with Bonnie. I caught him up on the latest.

"Tom," I asked, "don't you think Jesus would be on *my* side in this?"

"No," he said. "Jesus is busy with his own stuff, and is not going to get involved in your little tug-of-war. Plus, don't forget, he has his own mother to deal with. She's all he can handle, as far as mothers go. Also, she is completely dressed like a Muslim all the time, and he doesn't *ever* know what she's thinking."

November 12

I did not call Amy or Sam today, because I was too mental and angry. I tried to tend to my own emotional acre for a change, with a long hike in the hills with the dogs, three hours at the desk, twenty minutes of *Baba nam,* lunch with Millard at our favorite Thai place, and an afternoon binge of cable news,

Reese's Pieces, and a nap on the couch with the kitty. Also, *People* magazine, *Us,* and the *National Enquirer.* I bought some gourds and marigolds for my table, inspired by my framed photo of the guffawing woman and her wheelbarrow full of marigolds on the Day of the Dead in the hills of southern Mexico. I bought orange gourds because they are symbols of fertility, but also because they are dry. I feel very much like both these qualities — a big juicy grandma, a writer, and old and dry from crying yesterday during the worst of it. Gourds look like lights, warm and lovely, but they are filled with husks and seeds and they rattle when you shake them. I bought marigolds at Safeway that had been grown in a greenhouse. There's such molten sun in marigolds, such bitter fragrance, it gives you a little nose twist — I think their peculiar smell repels mosquitoes and other pests. They are very tough; it seems you could stomp on them and they would survive.

On the Day of the Dead, we go into the dark knowing that we are part of something huge, magnificent, and ancient. I have five or six Mexican *retablos,* small devotional paintings and hammered-tin reliefs, on my bookshelves, next to photos of my father, Sam, Jax, Clara. I love the playfulness and courage of skulls that grin, sunbathing skeletons, *mamacitas* making tortillas, little shards of professions — teachers, hookers, pianists — chalkboards, ermine wraps and beads, top hats.

November 13

This morning after prayers, and fifteen minutes of *Baba nam kevalam,* feeling very spiritually strong, I called Amy, and in this baby-doll Tweety Bird voice, I said I had heard that she was going to have the baby baptized in Chicago. She said that this was not true — that she and Sam wanted to have Jax baptized at St. Andrew, but not for a while, and then a second time at her grandmother's church in Chicago. She promised. She swore. "Of course we want to get him baptized where Sam got baptized." I started to splutter, "But but but, what about the date that's been set in Chicago — that you and your parents set, that our friend —" Then I dropped it. "Oh, I'm so glad," I said. "I wish I'd come to you right away." Then we laughed at my adorable foibles, and talked about what Jax was up to these days.

The thing is, I'm not sure I believe her. Or maybe my trust in her isn't deep enough to comfort me when it comes to something so vital.

But I *had* gotten the courage to release the scary secret to Amy out loud. Doing so felt huge and brave because of my terror that she might take the baby away again, or move away with him. Now there was one less ricochet factor, because I had come clean. I've always thought I could use my brain and my heart to jockey everyone around to the good. But life is not jockeyable. When you try, you make people infinitely crazier than they already were, including or especially yourself.

November 14

Amy came over for a marvelously uninteresting visit with Jax, which, after my mental turmoil yesterday, is more than welcomed.

Jax is over three and a half months old now, and is developing major mastery with his hands. He reaches for yours, and draws them to himself. Very industrious, a hardworking baby, gets your knuckles into his mouth so he can teethe on them, shoves his own hands and fingers into his mouth, copious Newfoundland drool, bubbles.

Why does he spend most of his time shoving his hands into his mouth?

Because he can. It must feel fabulous, and

his work is to practice coordination skills and aim, by putting stuff — i.e., you — into his mouth, and he doesn't hurt himself, doesn't jam his fingers into his eyes. He aims for the mouth, and the hand goes in. He has a system.

November 16

Jax has gone bad. Now instead of just reaching for your hands to shove into his mouth or to study, he reaches for your rings. He holds on to them! You can see the little wheels in his mind turning! He also does bracelets and watches; he's in gypsy mode. Watch your wallet.

November 17

I invited Millard over to celebrate Jax's four-month birthday a few days early, and then decided to make a party of it, because Jax has so many cousins in Chicago, and in a kind of Kim Jong Il gesture, I wanted a display of West Coast cousinly grandeur. I invited my first cousin Ricky, Millard's son; Ricky's teenage son, Oliver, who is Jax's second cousin, or first cousin twice removed, or something; my brother Stevo and his six-year-old, Clara, who is Sam's cousin, so Jax's cousin once removed; and then cousin Neshama. I got one-bite cupcakes, vanilla with confetti sprinkles; chips and guacamole; and big, fat red grapes.

Millard came first, somehow both handsome and spectral, and Amy arrived not long after. She is really looking regal these days, bearing the gift of Jax to Millard, like the Magi. She has finally introduced Jax to food, rice cereal and banana, which is a big step, and I am proud of her.

Jax is becoming part of the world now, noticing an area with a much bigger periphery than before; and he seems to feel that this world is a safe place. Ha.

Stevo and Clara arrived, and fought for possession of Jax, like he was a football. She is such a piece of sunshine, tall for her age, impish, stylish.

The dogs lick and lick Jax, because he is a horizontal animal, too; they think he's theirs. We call them the granddogs. They are giving him a great immune system, with those big tongues and heavy breath. It's got to be good for him — we are not in the slums of Rio, and I don't think we have hookworm here. Although maybe I should call the CDC in the morning.

Who would have thought that Amy and I would be celebrating Jax's four-month birthday together, here, at my house, with Millard, Ricky, Oliver, Stevo, Clara, and Neshama? Maybe it's better if I don't call the CDC, and instead savor these sweet afternoons as much as I can, like one-bite cupcakes.

November 24
Amy dropped Jax off so she could do some errands. I got to give him a bottle of milk she had pumped, and rock him to sleep. I couldn't stop thinking about Amy after she left. She has a purposeful chugging quality that I associate with women in Mexico. She is a good mother, with great stubbornness, playfulness, and total propriety. The meta-message is, Yes, you can hold and play with my baby, but he is MINE. He's my baby.

She has so grown into this role. She looks less undone, more pulled together, prepared.

Neshama said, after watching Amy and me together at the party, that I was sweet and tender with her, judiciously held back. She said I'm like a cheerful social worker. I'm cautious, because Amy is a fierce bull-dozer, and I am Thomas the Tank Engine. Sometimes I push into where her dark places are, and she gets cold and hard — as at the end of her pregnancy, when she casually skipped the meeting with her doctor, and I got so uptight, even though it was her

111

body, her doctor, her health insurance. Oh — and her baby.

I keep opening myself to her, offering to do anything I can to help, or carry the burden, but she says, with her body language, This is where I am, and who I am, and whose baby this is, and how it is going to be. I admire that she faces me with matriarchal authority, but she's twenty! So I'm experiencing a little cognitive dissonance.

November 24

I was forced by the strain of my condition to call Bonnie late last night. She is raising two grandchildren of her own, as her youngest daughter, their mother, sometimes simply disappears and lives on the streets. Bonnie stays up till midnight so she can have a few hours to herself after the kids are put to bed. I caught her up.

"Dearest, maybe Jax *should* be baptized in Chicago," she said. "Who knows?

"And besides, the spiritual truth is that Jax is already baptized — he was at the very moment of his birth. He is life, God getting God's self born again, and the baptism is just to *consecrate* that. I know, honey, I hear you: You want to consecrate that at St. Andrew. So it's okay for you

112

to ask for what you need and want, and then try to be a good sport if you don't get your way.

"It's Sam and Amy's decision. And it's very important stuff — between *them.* This exact mess is the very place where God is. Of course it's much easier to know this in a Zen garden. If they baptize Jax in Chicago, just know that it will work out entirely for the good. Don't be a big baby — if it is held there, you will go, and you will behave with generosity and elegance. Don't judge or withhold from Ray or Trudy just because you don't get your way. These are Jax's *grandparents* we're talking about, for God's sake. This is a sacred contract that Jax made as he came into the world — bless the grandparents and be grateful and full of wonder that this delicious, juicy baby who got himself born is big and stretchy enough to include all three of you. Trudy, you, and Ray. And it is okay if you were pissy. We bless the full expression.

"Amy is trying to express something, about her roots, her other home — and Sam and Amy need to learn this as a couple. Every story is always about the prodigal son and the prodigal daughter. So welcome Amy back, over and over again. Welcome her home. I know, I know — you'll never call me again. But I will be up another half-hour if you need me."

November 26

Thanksgiving was perfect, with Millard and his four grown kids; grandson Oliver and granddaughters Freya and Daphne; Stevo and his fiancée, Annette; Annette's grown daughter, Rachel; Sam and Amy and Jax; assorted riffraff from church and recovery. My cooking, if possible, gets worse with age, but Millard and his kids are excellent cooks. Amy made a great chocolate cake, with a colorful turkey on it, made by tracing the palm of her hand with a tube of frosting, fingers outstretched, which she learned to do when she was ten, and which cannot be improved upon. She and Sam bickered a little, which I don't mind much right now, because she is such a good mother. Sam fell asleep on my bed, and Jax in my arms after Amy nursed him. He was rosy and unde-manding and at full comfort. After I was sure he was sleeping soundly, I touched the flush of his cheeks in that light brown skin and traced those bold eyebrows. Of course, like all babies, he wakes up with a startle, slightly groping and low-level graspy, but with no sense of a time bomb about to go off. The beauty of the curve of his head —

how it rests in the crook of my elbow —
almost makes me want to flog myself, out
of a desperate, unbearable love. All grandparents I've mentioned this to have felt this.
He's a Fibonacci spiral, like a nautilus shell
— one of those patterns in mathematical
expression with a twisting eternal perfection.

*November 27, Letter to Jax on the Secret
of Life*

Dear Jax: Yesterday was your first Thanksgiving, and it is time for me to impart to
you the secret of life. You will go through
your life thinking there was a day in second
grade that you must have missed, when the
grown-ups came in and explained *everything*
important to the other kids. They said:
"Look, you're human, you're going to feel
isolated and afraid a lot of the time, and
have bad self-esteem, and feel uniquely
ruined, but here is the magic phrase that
will take this feeling away. It will be like a
feather that will lift you out of that fear and
self-consciousness every single time, all
through your life." And then they told the
children who were there that day the magic
phrase that everyone else in the world
knows about and uses when feeling blue,
which only you don't know, because you

were home sick the day the grown-ups told the children the way the whole world works.

But there was not such a day in school. No one got the instructions. That is the secret of life. Everyone is flailing around, winging it most of the time, trying to find the way out, or through, or up, without a map. This lack of instruction manual is how most people develop compassion, and how they figure out to show up, care, help and serve, as the only way of filling up and being free. Otherwise, you grow up to be someone who needs to dominate and shame others, so no one will know that you weren't there the day the instructions were passed out.

I know exactly one other thing that I hope will be useful: that when electrical things stop working properly, ninety percent of the time you can fix them by unplugging the cord for two or three minutes. I'm sure there is a useful metaphor here.

November 28
Today there was a tick from the dogs on Jax's foot, or rather, on the feet of his jammies. I hate ticks. They represent all that is wrong with the world, all that is nasty, disgusting, random, and vicious. It looked like an innocent black spot, a tiny black

sesame seed, at first, and I moved forward to get it, and it moved. It carried so much dread for me that it may as well have been a snake. You try to be so vigilant, and where does it get you? You can't be vigilant enough. Now it feels like "The Masque of the Red Death" around here.

I suppose, though, since Jax is always getting dressed and undressed and patted and bathed and dressed again, at the very worst a tick would be discovered quickly.

Neshama once told me about a friend of hers who had to be treated for parasites after visiting a foreign country, and the doctors also had to give her meds to kill the ticks that came with the parasites, *on* the parasites.

I ask you.

I felt upon remembering this that I could not go on. How do any of our kids live? I know lots of people with Lyme disease now. They get a tick bite, or they don't even notice it until the ticks become swollen and spongy, or eventually, and most horribly, like the teeny balls of mercury from broken thermometers we used to roll around in our hands that would pill back together into one ball.

In the old days, when I was a kid, we always tried using matches to make the ticks back out, or nail polish or petroleum, which I think they secretly love: they huffed it and burst into song — "I feel pretty! Oh, so pretty!" — and didn't budge.

It feels awful not to be able to protect Jax from so much, but you can't bog down in that, because then you'd be frozen, and of no hope or help to anyone. And that frozen hopelessness is the welcome mat for the Red Death. Come on in! Put your feet up.

Right before bed, Amy called full of excitement to say that Jax can now roll over whenever he wants. We laughed and were joyful together about what a strong little champion he is, and how hilarious. I said I couldn't wait to see this for myself.

But what I thought was: Now he can roll right over onto those ticks.

November 30
Yesterday was the first Sunday of Advent, so in the afternoon after church, I e-mailed my dear friend Bill Rankin, the Episcopal priest who helped fish me out of the waters of alcoholism almost twenty-four years ago. Now he is one of my best friends. I wrote, "Tell me your understanding of Advent."

He wrote back, "Dearest Annie: To the best of my knowledge Advent was a season cooked up by the church to add drama and, as it were, spiritual foreplay before Xmas. Since it had to have an outwardly holy purpose, it was advertised as a season of self-examination and repentance in preparation for the incarnation of the deity, so in the 'liturgical' churches, like the Romans and the Episcopalians, the clergy wear purple albs around their shoulders — a supposedly somber (serious) color — as opposed to the red they wear for saints' days and the white they wear for Christmas, Easter, weddings and funerals.

"Implicit in Advent is the no-fun-at-all searching of the self in order to repent of all the sins, shortcomings, errors, screw-ups, and omissions that the childish think should be taken care of before coming face-to-face with The Holy.

"My own view, since you asked, is that the church strives in Advent to make a large deal out of a fairly small idea. I remember that years ago a professor in seminary said that the hardest sermons to preach are the Advent ones. I wasn't with it enough to ask him why, but all these decades later I think his meaning was something like this: The church says we should engage in serious self-examination for four long weeks, since Jesus is coming. It's hard for a preacher to make that message interesting or consequential, especially for four weeks. So typically the churches have shrunk the object of these words to sex, have done so for millennia: it sure helps keep people's attention. Micro-ethics, micro-spirituality. What a bore.

"The churches have no desire or courage to take on the evils that matter — greed, poverty, racism, militarism — so the experience of Advent ends up being bland, tedious, and, I frequently think, empty.

"That's my sinful two cents' worth. You owe me lunch. When might I expect it? Love, Bill."

December 1, Interview with Sam
Sam was talking over the phone about how powerfully connected he still feels to his grandmother Gertrud, who died a year ago, so I decided to turn this into an interview:

"Our connection could never be severed," he said, "even by her dying, and even though we weren't pumping family blood — because the connection was never physical. And sever means physical. But I was just a boy who needed a grandma. I miss her like a child would, not a man, and every day.

"With Jax's birth, Samland has been permanently breached. The entire time I was a teenager, I lived there, in my mind, but now there's no longer such a place. Now it's Sam-and-Jaxland. I'm still so close to being a teenager that I can remember how independent of you my choices were — and that's a scary epiphany: how completely independent of *my* needs and fears Jax's choices will be one day.

"We as parents have the illusion that we make our kids stronger, but they make us stronger.

"When he came into my life, it's like everything got intensely amplified — now school is lit by the force field of Jax, like having a new lighting system in your life.

"The illusion of control in your life is smashed. Sometimes when you're a parent you're just hanging on by a pinkie finger, and you say to God, 'Trusting you, Dude — I trust you have a plan for us.'

"I thought I could help Jax grow as strong as possible as a person, but he's in charge of how he decides to grow, or not. Like I was. I have three main ideas here I want to tell you about:

"It used to be kind of an accident that he could get his feet to his mouth, but now it's a tool in his movements. He grabs his feet to shift his weight forward, and to sit or roll. Now it's a lever, to use. He'll use his feet as a lever, as handles. He's discovered, 'Wow, they're attached to me. They have weight to them.' It's evolutionary, and it caught me by surprise because the foot phone seemed like a phase, but it was evolution — him starting the movement process, of rolling over, and rocking forward inch by inch, like someone with no arms. Now you can't take your eyes off him for a second. He'll go from being on his back to being on his stomach, with an arm trapped beneath him, and hurt himself. Now if you look away, he can get hurt.

"Another thing is that I see now that all Jax needs is loving care, and diaper changes. All he needs to grow are opportunities to figure things out. He needs us to spend enough time with him on his back so he can learn to arch it. He gets bigger and stronger every day regardless of us, instead of because of us. He *is* life, he's life learning to seize itself. He's like a snowball at the top of a hill, gathering himself as he rolls. He's his own snowball, made of the same snow as us, and life. Like, look at me, even with a dad, it shows you that you need God to be breathing into you — that your parents just need to be guardians and protectors, because you're your own snowball.

"And third, he makes me stronger, because you have to balance so much now — you have to reschedule everything you have to do — homework and him. It forces you to tap into more of you than you knew was there — parts that you didn't even know you had.

"With him in the equation, everything is a small victory, just getting homework done is a small miracle, because part of my mind has to be on him, lying on the ground playing, even as I try to study. Before, it was like I was trying to keep four plates spinning in the air, with just Amy and regular homework and life — now it's four plates, *and* something precious and priceless and fragile in the air, in the mix, *and* at the same time a Ming dynasty monkey that is able to animate itself and try to escape from the air where you are trying to keep it in the juggling lineup.

"Now I get my laundry done, and it's WOW. Or I finish my homework, and I can hear the sound track from *Chariots of Fire* playing.

"I'm getting more resilient as a father, about doing things I don't want to do — the self-centered person is still totally there, even though I'm a father figure. There used to be a list of stuff I hoped to get done, homework or exercise or whatever, and now if I want to make a schedule for myself, it's like, 'Thanks for sharing,' because instead, I know I'm going to need to stare at my son for a long time. Or I might have to call Amy and find out exactly what he's doing, if they are at home and I am at school.

"When I can put a picture of him in my head, it's in real time — I'm not relying on memories to see him inside myself. I can be a fly on the wall watching right as it happens, even if we are miles apart, like I'm watching a live feed, because he and I are connected in my bones. It's completely like with Gertrud, because with that deep a connection, that transcends death, it's like wireless Internet versus one of those old coiled-up phone cords. There's not a physical cord that connects you — it's in the soul and your body. Gertrud can be there for me in a second flat if I need her. If Jax and I didn't see each other for twenty years, we'd recognize each other instantly. It's like *Namaste* or *Namaskar* — like, I recognize divinity in you, but actually more like, I recognize our each-otherness; instantly.

"I love my dad. But he couldn't invest in me when I was little, when I was a young company. He could have a strong young man who was seriously there in his life, and on his side now, as he's older, seventy, but

124

he didn't invest. I think about him and care for him, but he's there, and I'm here. With Jax."

December 3, Interview with Sam
"I got no sleep the last couple of nights, and I feel so fucked up. I don't know what to do. I don't know what to do. I got no sleep and I have tons of homework, and I cannot believe God has a plan. It's so bad today — not manic bad, just hopeless and weighted, and I'm exhausted, and it's all over. I feel there is NO plan for me and Amy. Is there *any* way to make this work? We fight, and it gets so supercharged because of this kid. It's about nothing at all, but we get so emotional and we're each afraid the other is going to do something drastic.

"Sometimes I want the looseness of what life used to be like. When I could have just gone to Mexico and lived in a shack on nothing.

"Now I'd have to take Jax or leave him, and I couldn't leave him — and I can't take him from his mom. I feel trapped and powerless and out of control and insane, but I've lost my mind to the point where I can just look at all the bad things and laugh like a maniac, like when a homework assignment gets destroyed in the computer and I laugh because it's so pathetic and hopeless and absurd.

"And I have no choice of plans but to keep moving forward."

It blew my mind to hear Sam express himself at this level of self-awareness and humility. It made me feel like I must have done something right. What recurred to me all day were his three words, "We as parents." I needed to make room inside myself for this equating, the way I would make room on a crowded shelf for a new book.

December 4

I woke up with the idea that Sam's thoughts are like reading very plain modern versions of the psalms: "I love this! It's great! My heart soars! I will try to be worthy of this gift. Wait. Now I am doomed. I can't believe this is the way it's supposed to be. I hate everything and don't have a shred of faith. Oh, wait, yes I do — now I remember. Thank you, God. Back in the saddle."

December 5

Amy and Jax came over, and Amy and I watched a vampire movie. Awake or asleep, Jax is a work of art. I think he is very advanced for four months and two weeks:

he laughs, squeals, bubbles away, recognizes his name, turns toward sounds — the phone ringing, the kitty screaming with outrage that Bodhi has licked her, Bodhi's yelp when the kitty claws him, Lily in the role of martyred wife; why can't we all just get along? Jax can track the animals. He laughs, and he lifts his arms to be picked up. Maybe he thinks the mood at the petting zoo has soured. Better get out while you can.

So between the vampires and the bubbling and the pets milling around like extras, our dance card was already pretty full when the mailman arrived. He delivered the Christmas ornaments Amy had ordered online. I remembered giving her my credit card number a couple of months ago, so that she could buy them and therefore wouldn't want to take Jax and move away. I had a pang when I saw the online bill, though — if you don't have money, why not make popcorn or cranberry necklaces, and paper snowflakes, like the March girls would have done?

But the ornaments made me so happy today. There were two of them, one commemorating Amy's paternal grandmother, Jessie, and one memorializing Gertrud, in enameled picture frames with each one's name, date of death, holly and ivy, and hearts. In the picture on Sam's ornament, Gertrud is holding him near a Christmas tree. She is about seventy, he is sixteen months, and they are studying the branches together. Her hair is silky and European, snowy white, and his towheaded blond, nearly white, too.

I was holding Jax asleep in my arms while Amy unwrapped the ornaments. I saw the delighted-child side of her, the other side of the coin of the iron will that brought us Jax. I saw her pleasure in the ornaments, and her profound love of the grandparent who is dead — perhaps this explains her holding out for the baptism at the other grandma's church — an otherworldly connection she has to her ancestors; she honors them by remembering them, calling them into the present. She honors her living grandmother by visiting her with Jax in Chicago. These relationships are a major part of who she is.

I can perfectly remember how she took biblical care of Gertrud, at Sam's nineteenth-birthday party here, when Millard, only four years younger than Gertrud, seemed like Mary Lou Retton in comparison. It was Gertrud's last outing. Amy sat close to her, holding water for her in silence, taking away her plate when Gertrud was finished, without being asked, like an old man's wife. I thought of Ruth and Naomi. After Gertrud stopped going out, Amy started the home beauty salon visits, which she kept up faithfully the entire last year of Gertrud's life.

"Jessie" is tattooed on a huge cross on Amy's upper back: she still grieves the loss. Still not sure about the "Jax" part. Amy and Sam said they like the sound of it, and when Millard recently asked Sam if it was short for "Ajax," of *Iliad* fame, Sam said yes, partly, but that mostly they liked the way it sounded.

I said to Amy as she unwrapped the ornaments, "Promise me three things. You'll never get him a Nintendo, let him go off to war, or let him ride motorcycles," and she promised on the spot, although within the hour she had reneged on the motorcycle clause.

December 7
Yesterday was the second Sunday of Advent. The days are dark and short, and life has been dark and scary, with so many bad things happening to people I love. Tom has been having a difficult patch, and we meet at the church of IKEA as often as possible, because it is equidistant from our houses and always cheers us up. Yesterday I asked,

"In your depression, and with so many people having such a hard time, where is Advent?"

He tried to wiggle out of it by saying, "You Protestants and your little questions!"

Then, when pushed, he said: "Faith is a decision. Do we believe we are ultimately doomed and fucked and there's no way out? Or that God and goodness make a difference? There is heaven, community, and hope — and hope that there is life beyond the grave."

"But Tom, at the same time, the grave is very real, dark and cold and lonely."

"Advent is not for the naive. Because in spite of the dark and cold, we see light — you look up, or you make light, with candles, or with strands of lightbulbs on trees.

"And you give light. Beauty helps, in art and nature and faces. Friends help. Solidarity helps. If you ask me, when people return phone calls, it's about as good as it gets. And who knows beyond that."

"But if you will try and tell me more, I will buy you Swedish meatballs."

"Meatballs, and dessert."

So over lunch at IKEA, he talked and I scribbled down notes: "Advent says that there is a way out of this trap — that we embrace our humanity, and Jesus' humanity, and then we remember that he is wrapped up in God. It's good to know where to find Jesus — in the least of these, among the broken, the very poor and marginalized. Jesus says, 'You want to see me? Look there.'

"Those tiny bits of connection to the broken are very real, and the kindness and attention people show to them create a bit of light. That's Advent. It's about *us*. It doesn't say, 'Glory to God and peace to me' — it says, 'Peace to people of goodwill.' I think some of us could work on goodwill, and when I talk to God about this later, I am not going to mention your name."

As I drove home that afternoon, I did notice the beautiful deciduous tree–lined streets of Marin, CGI-level flame-colored autumn leaves. In Larkspur, I saw a dozen snowy egrets in what must have been a very delicious meadow by the side of the road, and I had enough sense to pull over and sit and watch them eat for a while.

December 15
I want to collect my thoughts on what Jax is like, five days short of his being five months old. He is snuggled asleep in my arms, a miracle of function. Right now, we are a circuit of comfort and calm. He makes me

so much better than I am, the way Sam used to do.

My arm and his head are one unit. That's not going to last. This tiny guy contains such a huge, galumphy kid, who will unfurl, as we all have done, like those sponge animals that come in small capsules. In what feels like a year, he will be saying, "Nana, Nana, drop me off here," a block from school or the mall.

December 16

Our friend Olivia, who is fifteen, is back in the hospital with a flare-up of cystic fibrosis. I met her on the third day of her life, when I was babysitting her older sister, who was five at the time, and engaged to Sam. I have always adored Olivia, and we have lifted her in prayer at St. Andrew every Sunday for fourteen years, along with a sick boy in Wisconsin who has kidney tumors. She is beautiful, blond, a champion gymnast, and has attentive, calm parents and cutting-edge doctors with a great sense of humor, and churches around the country praying for her, and I used to find solace in all that.

That, however, was before I became a grandparent. Now I am often angry with God about the sick kids we know. "What can you *possibly* be thinking?" I ask, but get no reply; not a clue. And if perfect, mellow, lovely baby Olivia could turn out to have CF, then all bets are off. No one is safe, period. I know that if anything happened to Jax, it would be a dizzying and primary loss, not once removed, but involving also the devastation of seeing my child having to try to survive the end of the world. Ten years ago, an old writer friend and his wife told me that they had recently lost their grandson in a bike accident, and my reaction was entirely about their poor daughter, the child's mother. Until Jax, I didn't get it, that they had lost a great love of their own and had a grown child who was in permanent grief beyond all imagining.

Olivia's father called today and asked if I could visit her at the hospital in San Francisco. She and her mom had made the room their own, and we had a few perfect hours together. She is so healthy — well, except for the cystic fibrosis — mobile and fully alive and lovely. She is a miracle, even with a cough that worsens over time, and in fine fettle today.

I brought her photos of Jax, and lots of colors of clay and beads, and we made Christmas-tree ornaments to give as presents, and we ate chocolates. That's all I know how to do — show up and ask God for help. Love and grace are bigger than the nightmare, supposedly. Without trusting this, we're doomed and ridiculous. Advent says that healing is coming here, and it will be okay. Chanukah says, Let there be light, and let it begin with me. It says, Even though it doesn't look like it, there will be enough oil to keep the lamps lit. Olivia's family is not religious, but they have been saved, literally, by the love of their friends since her diagnosis, and by the presence of her grandparents. When she was Jax's age, no one knew there was anything wrong, let alone cystic fibrosis.

Children should not have treacherous diseases or be afraid. This should be the one rule we all agree on.

December 17

Amy left me with a bottle of breast milk and went out to do errands. I had Jax for two hours all to myself. We gazed at each other. I chatted him up. He bubbled back at me, squealed, laughed when I did silly things. Then I put him in his new office, a bouncy saucer/home entertainment center I got at the baby consignment store, which he stands in (dear God) to perform various clickety-clack activities with balls and beads and mirrors and teethers.

He's huge and tiny — huge in how big and healthy he has grown, huge in his effect on our lives and psyches, even as he is not much bigger than my cat. Time has flown like a falcon: he was nine pounds, and now, in a blink, he's almost twenty pounds. Amy came back from shopping for food and doing other errands in hunter-gatherer mode, busty and bustling. I could see that she was pleased with herself, but not crowing. I loved this moment. She did not have a single clutch when she saw the baby waking up surprised in my arms — she let me tend to him and help him find his sense of the familiar in me.

When he woke up, he instantly went for his fingers in his mouth — but not for Amy, even though he saw her. What a huge development for us all.

I had given Amy fifty dollars to buy some clothes at our great local consignment store, to feel good and womanly and warm and pretty in, and she modeled these for both of us. Jax looked around calmly, and she was calm, too, not needing to cling and be all over him. He's secure for now in whoever he is. I guess that when you can get your hand into your mouth when you need it, and you have a tool for self-comfort, you're halfway home.

They hung around for another hour. I love that Amy feels so safe and less alone here at my house.

December 19

I made a fire in the fireplace, lit a couple of candles, and arranged three small bouquets of freesias in a vase, to make a flame of flowers, yellow, red, white. Sam called to say that Jax is like a cat burglar now. Any seat you put him in, he starts studying how it works, and how you've secured him in place, so he can make a break. He cases the joint. If you look away, he feverishly continues the mission.

"We could always see the gears turning — we're his parents, after all," Sam said. "But now the gears are making new connections, and those connections move down his neck from his brain to his arms and his hands."

I can still see Sam when he was Jax's age and became a cat burglar, and now I see how intricate designs and illustrations flow from the lead of his pencil.

December 21

Sam called to say that Jax had held his bottle by himself for the first time. He's nearly ready for a paper route.

It's Amy's twenty-first birthday today.

They are having a real babysitter tonight, our friend Danielle, who is my hairdresser, so they can go to Fisherman's Wharf and have dinner at Joe's Crab Shack. I guess they just don't *care* about the baby anymore. Otherwise, they would have left him with me.

December 24
We are going to celebrate Christmas Eve at Sam and Amy's apartment in the city; Stevo, Annette, her daughter, Rachel, and Clara will meet us there. Clara will be seven in two weeks. I remember when she was Jax's age, eighteen months ago. Now, in the aftermath of divorce, she has hit the lottery: a sweet, beautiful stepmother, two adoring new grandparents where there had been none, and an out-of-thin-air twenty-year-old sister who is a connoisseur of hair clips, glittery jewelry, and floral headbands. God is totally showing off again.

Amy bought a ham the size of a bulldog, for seven of us. She will be cooking it all day. The rest of us will bring salads, desserts, and sides. We'll open presents after dinner. I'm giving Sam and Amy big checks, Clara a misty-green Stella McCartney taffeta skirt, and Jax the greatest toys that Marin had to offer, some made by craftspeople, which he'll love when he has children — "My Nana gave me this hand-carved locomotive my first Christmas. I've kept it all this time" — and some plastic, great educational toys that are loud, good for sucking and smashing *now*.

At midnight, Sam, Amy, and Jax will leave on a red-eye to visit her parents in North Carolina for nine days.

I'm sure I'll be just fine.

New Year's Eve

I went to dinner and the movies with Doug, and dearest friends Bill and Emmy Smith, and was in bed with a book by eleven. So it was just right, and the week since the kids left has been, too. Nothing of interest has occurred, which is par for the course in my case, and I have savored my rich and un-eventful daily life — walks with the dogs and friends, work, reading, a nap, more reading, a few get-togethers. I have a new perspective on spiritual abundance, thanks to my friend Michelle, who told me about going to Starbucks the other day for a pecan sticky bun.

She normally doesn't order pastry at Starbucks, because it's fattening, but the other day she decided to treat herself to a pecan sticky bun. She spent quite a lot of time picking out the exact one she wanted, which meant the one with the most pecans. She pointed it out to the counter person. He had to move a few others that were in the way, so she took her coffee and sat down.

He brought the sticky bun over, all wrapped up and on a plate. She started taking it out of the paper, and instantly saw that it was the wrong bun, not the one she had chosen. This one had only three pecans on top. She wrapped it back up and walked to the counter, where she pointed this out to the young man, with crisp annoyance. He looked at her incredulously. "Lady," he said, "turn it over."

And on the other side, the bun was tiled with candied pecans.

January 3

Sam, Amy, and Jax got back last night, and Jax is a new creation. He's talking. Sam called to say they were all coming over, and to prepare myself: "It's like he suddenly got new software. His efforts at talking now are shades of gray, instead of just screaming or crying. He has a new arsenal of noises he can make. Like someone who has taken a massive amount of sedative and can't make words but has strong opinions. They're like dolphin sounds, little creature noises. Lots

139

of *eeee*. The fart noise is used pretty creatively — he can do a new angry face now by incorporating fart noises, like the French soldier in *Monty Python and the Holy Grail* who says, 'I fart in your general direction.' And sometimes he's just doing it to listen to it. These are the greatest hits, the farting noises, dolphins, *eeee*s." I remembered when Sam could first make these sounds, always most loudly in church, of course, and loudest of all during the congregation's silent prayers. It's funny, those things that sanctify community life.

January 5

Sam and I took turns watching Jax while Amy went to the chiropractor. Jax drinks from his bottle like a wino with a bottle of Night Train. His tongue lolls out when he gets a good hit, and then he starts sucking fiercely again. According to Sam, he's saying, "All I need is one more slug of that, baby. Just to take the edge off."

Or as my friend Don used to say about his first morning drink, just to get all the flies going in one direction.

He was fussier than usual, as his front teeth are coming in, and he was filibustering most of our offerings, of toys, carpet time, peekaboo.

January 5

Millard is losing weight before our very eyes. It is clear that he is dying, but my cousins do not want to call hospice, which is to me the next course of action. This would mean admitting that the end is not too far down the road; my cousins are not ready for that yet. They make it seem like I am hysterical and overreacting when I suggest this.

It is funny how no one seems to want my always excellent advice.

He needs a full-time nurse in case he falls, because his son Ricky, with whom he lives, is gone all day, at work. He needs help in the shower, and will need morphine soon for the pain. My cousins do what my brothers and I did when my dad was sick but still lucid: make jokes and hope for the best. For instance, today when no one was looking, Millard fished his car keys out of the drawer where someone had hidden them, and drove himself to town. My cousin Robby, Millard's eldest, called to say, "We've got a runner."

I laughed, but this triggers me: My dad sneaked off a few times in the car after his license had been taken away because of his seizures — and there are so many small kids in our neighborhood.

Robby called back an hour later to say, "He just got back from the store with four bags of groceries. He's okay, he just wants to provide for his family. You Christians are always trying to bury people early." This completely hurt my feelings, until I remembered that I have to let them deal in their own way with the trampoline of a family whose patriarch is dying. They are the ones who are going to have to do all the weird work that has to be done at the end of someone's life, and I have to release Millard to them. If they ask, I can help. Period.

What a concept.

January 6
It is foggy, and everyone is in post-holiday hangover, especially me.

I hiked in the hills early this morning with Karen and my dogs.

I said, "What does this fog look like to you?"

"Hopelessness."

"I mean, physically?"

"Like the world has glaucoma."

We were way high up, in a thick fog. It looked like God had thrown a dove-gray cashmere blanket over our cage. But the beauty was that you'd been spared having to see too far ahead. Only here, only now, only a few dozen feet in any direction.

It was tragic and romantic, very *Wuthering Heights.* Karen looked unusually pretty — but who doesn't look better with a scarf draped over the lightbulb? The flaws and imperfections go away.

Instead of the usual feeling you have up here, like you're the Little Prince standing on the earth, looking out at an endless expanse of sky and universes, it was like being under a lid or a dome. And everywhere we went — on the road, on trails, up a steep green hill — the dome followed directly above us.

January 6, Interview with Sam
"Hi, Mom. We have a new development. If you include Jax in the conversation, like first saying something while *not* talking to him, and then saying it again to him — 'Jax, isn't the sky blue?' — this makes him laugh.

"Also, sneaking up on him makes him laugh.

"I don't love the crying, but I guess it's part of the package. I've gotten better at letting the noises go on without cringing — like when he just has to cry it out. I'm a designer, so I want there to be a solution to everything — he's crying, there must be something wrong, and fixable — but we're learning that he needs to cry it out. To discharge all the accumulated energy.

"He hates to go to sleep, like he's missing out, and he fights it. At bedtime, he knows the jig is up. We try to let him cry and tire himself out. This is new to me, and the hardest thing a parent can do. Every nerve in your body wants to move to his side and console him, and not make him be alone or unhappy ever again, for even a second. We crack under the strain."

I told Sam about when he was three months old, and Pammy came over at night to support me in letting him learn to cry himself to sleep. His stomach was now big enough to hold enough milk for eight hours, but he had developed the habit of waking up every four hours to nurse and check in with me on stuff he might have missed while sleeping.

The baby book said to put him down, pat his back, and not pick him up, no matter how piteous he sounded. I was committed to letting him cry it out, for however long it took, and I made Pammy promise to help me keep my butt on the couch, like Ulysses strapped to the mast.

I lasted close to six minutes, then did crack under the strain and picked him up. Ulysses had an unfair advantage over me:

the mast, and wax in his ears.

All willingness to change comes from pain, and it wasn't for another month of psycho-exhaustion that Pammy and I tried again. Then it took only three or four nights.

Sam: "This is a point in my life when I need God to have a plan, because I don't have a plan. I don't have any idea of where this is all going. I keep finding this trust and surrender to take the next right step, because I don't have a choice. I can be miserable and controlling, or I can trust and surrender — like when Amy told me in November of 2008 that she was pregnant and keeping the baby; well, after a few awful days, I saw that either I could be a pain-in-the-ass no-show, or I could understand that history was being made. Every day, this little guy — who *was* going to get born — was growing a little bit more ready for life, so I decided I would love him sight unseen as he grew inside Amy. So I did have a choice.

"I'm grateful that I have these two people to completely put love energy into, even if things are not perfect between me and Amy, if Jax is demanding or is getting a tooth — I can stand it better, that things are unendingly hard and loud. It's like a spiritual skin-hardening — like my skin is toughen-

145

ing up, and not just the hands and the high-traffic areas.

"The price of all this love energy is the tremendous burden and self-sacrifice and total hundred-eighty-degree overhaul of your life. Some people live a bachelor life their whole life and either do or don't love it, but they aren't forced into doing spiritual weightlifting and aerobics, as I am by Jax and school. I think God needs me to master this level of hardship for what is coming. One good thing is that this year, people didn't even want to say their excuses in front of me, because on top of what we are all doing collectively at school, I'm also raising a baby. I'm doing what they're doing in school and what they used to complain about, and also doing this other job, of being a father. So my peers are seeing that you can get a lot more done than you would have ever imagined, if you have to, and they have the choice to rise to that level. I am showing up every day like a raggedy, pathetic soldier, shell-shocked with exhaustion, like part of my uniform and hat are blown away, but I stagger to the lab or the shop where all the materials are, the saws and drills and equipment and resins and paint booths and foam blocks and clay and fiberglass. And my friends feel like, If Sam can get to the shop, with Jax and Amy at home, with all those huge needs, then what possible excuse can I have to blow it off?

"Maybe I'm growing up because I don't have the choice not to. I couldn't say to God, 'Look, I *want* to grow up into manhood, but the timing on this isn't good.'

"I see the hardest patches as stepping-stones for what I will need as I go out from here."

January 7

Sam's tuition and my quarterly income taxes are both due now, but I found out today that I am getting a check from my publisher this week. I told Sam and he said, "Thank you, Riverhead Books, for employing the unemployable."

I did not tell a soul that I was feeling so anxious about our finances. If you get too tweaked about money, it means you have bad values, and you feel like a shit for caring so much, and it gets you at a deep level, down to the bone — your greed, and superficiality, all sense of worth and safety.

When you don't have enough or you run out, you feel in your core that the leak has begun and there will be no end to the leakage. And this makes you feel like a chump. Whereas having some money gives you the conviction that you're not naked in the howling wind, even though you basically are, existentially. It assures you that at least you're better than some people — you're not with the crack addicts or, maybe even worse, living with the relatives. So there's that.

Everything in the culture supports the illusion that if you get the right products, spouse, and house, and keep your weight down in general, the real you will not be exposed, and people may be able to love you — horrible you.

But the winds of opinion or the bus or cancer can still mow you down, equally, whether you have money or not. Money can't even protect you from baldness. Many of the richest, most powerful men in the world are bald, and all the money in the world can't prevent or reverse this. There's no treatment you can buy, even with your millions. Rogaine helps a few men, a little. You'd think there would be *something* you could do if money was no object — some advanced procedure, in São Paulo, involving gene-splicing with a hairy monkey. But no.

January 7
Wow.

After all those uncomfortable patches

we've come through, we had a delayed, lovely, just fine twenty-first-birthday party for Amy at my house, with Neshama, Stevo, and Clara, who manages to be exultant and shy; my cousin Robby, Emmy Smith, Sam, Amy, Jax.

Sam has been out of school for two weeks. He's a different person.

Jax was a fully shared human being today. Amy released him to the tribe, and everyone clamored for a turn to hold him.

Sam's tickling Jax as a means of happy contact seems redundant, because Jax is all smiles, laughs, and connection. Still, this image, whenever I witness it, breaks my heart.

For the first time in months, Sam, though weary, showed real flexibility and ease, maybe even a little bounce. For once he was not trapped in "Oh God, I should really be doing something else," or "I'm dying, I need to get some sleep, I have so much to do."

I was blown away by everyone, especially Sam and Amy — it's all kind of a mess sometimes between them, but today was what love looks like. Sam was on time, wearing a clean dress shirt and jeans, occasional joy on his face in seeing Amy honored. I know he'd rather be out and about, cruising with his friends, with the guys, after the last three grinding weeks of projects and finals. But he is here, in the midst of the love of our friends and family, and just so totally present after having been away.

Love looks like kindness.

Love also looks like the cake Robby made for Amy, the best cake I've ever had. It was three layers of dark chocolate, with a cooked buttercream frosting. It was chewy and resistant, but it melted in your mouth at the same time, don't ask me how. It was a perfect metaphor for life, the light and the dark together, several textures at once.

And it wasn't pretty at all.

I don't trust pretty. Petit fours are pretty, but they're always a little sawdusty.

The cake looked like the earth. When you cut through the top layer of frosting, though, it was like looking into a hole in the snow and seeing dark dirt below — out of such homeliness came the sublime, which pretty much sums up most of life these days.

The frosting coated every raw place in you, like an emollient or an unguent. And it wasn't too sweet. There was no gritty sugar feel that would make your teeth crunkle.

It had a funny crust, like a protective layer, and did not have a perky shape: the three layers weren't stacked exactly right. It looked like a Dr. Seuss cake.

Cute cakes squash down too fast. I'm not saying I couldn't eat a whole one all by myself, and they are reduced to dope-rush-sweet even as you chew — which, don't get me wrong, I like. But you could have fed Robby's cake to the Queen of England, and it was so great he made it for Amy's twenty-first-birthday party and Jax's five-month, even though Jax preferred to eat the plate and Lily's ear.

January 7
I bought a used mini-laptop, an Asus, on eBay to take to India with me, and it was hilariously tiny, and sophisticated. But when I went into Borders to check out the Wi-Fi, it didn't work. I spent an hour on my cell phone with a technical support person at Asus, but she could not figure out the problem and get it working. She suggested that I mail it to the company. But I was leaving in a few days. So I called Sam from the car, feeling distraught, duped, ripped off. I'd bought another lemon, which must mean that *I'm* a lemon.

"Now, Mom," he said sternly, "what is the first thing we do?" I didn't have a clue, unless it was to assign blame. "We seek wise counsel. You call Rachel after we hang up." Rachel is the IT person who always fixes our computers.

"I know the feeling," he said. He reminded me about his buying a used paintball gun for several hundred dollars when he was fourteen. All of his friends in eighth grade had them, and went to special sites in the woods where they shot each other with ammo balls of paint. (Eighth grade was only six years ago. Eighth grade. God almighty. I need to stop and put my head down between my knees.) Anyway, the gun was defective — but he couldn't get a refund, since it was used. So he started replacing it part by part. He said it was the Corvette of paintball guns. And three great things happened: He ended up with a much better piece of equipment. He could use it more effectively than the other kids could use theirs, because he knew every square inch of it and what each tiny part did. And after that he was able to help all of his friends with their paintball guns.

I went home and called Rachel. She completely knew this rare mini-computer because her husband had one, and she had worked on his. Of course. She fixed it that afternoon. Now I am the Steve Jobs of the Asus mini — I could take it apart in the dark and put it back together, like a Marine.

My favorite part of this whole experience

was the way the phone call with Sam ended. He said, "I know we're talking computers, but . . . As long as we're at it, there's something I've meant to tell you for a while. I think it might hurt your feelings." My stomach buckled.

"Okay," I said. "You can tell me."

"You need to talk to your friends about the style of jeans you wear."

"What?"

"Mom," he said calmly, gently. "I think you can do better."

January 9

I really don't need Jax anymore, since I have this fabulous mini-PC, but he and Amy came over this afternoon anyway. He has grown so long. And he's become both a danger to himself and a menace to society. He now focuses like a meth head on my necklaces and earrings, watching my ears with infinite wired patience. He flexes his fingers, warms them up like a safecracker, then grabs at my jewelry and holds on, while making farting noises.

Plus, Amy forgot to tell me, you can't leave paper around anymore. He's a paper eater. On their way back from North Carolina, Jax pooped out a zebra code.

"That fucking TSA," I said. "What next?"

No, Amy explained. While they were boarding in North Carolina, he sneakily ate the tag the airline had put on his stroller, which she and Sam were about to leave on the ramp to check. The bar code came out twenty-four hours later, perfectly formed, if worse for wear.

January 11
Jax is going to be six months old in nine days. I will be in India.

"Why are you going, again?" my friend Karen asked, as we walked in the hills early this the morning with my dogs. She said that when she thinks of India, she thinks poverty, poverty, poverty. And how absurd it is for Westerners to go there for an authentic spiritual experience, since you can have the same experience at the library. All you have to do is stop what you are doing, sit down, be solitary and present and breathe. And then you're there, in the eternal now.

I've dreamt of this my whole life; the desire to go to India has never lifted, and I can finally afford a ticket. I want the mosques, the temples, the lepers — in other words, the in-your-face experience. I guess I'm more of a Ganges-and-ghats type of gal.

"I couldn't handle the poverty, or the

sensory overload, and especially the jet lag," Karen said. "The way people look at each other at the thirteenth hour — it's the way you look at someone else who is in labor at the same time as you."

I have always been seeking God, direct experiences of truth or reality; so sue me. Because of the Beats and the Beatles and Ram Dass, I thought Truth was in India, or from that direction, instead of wherever my butt was.

"It's Nana's Excellent Adventure," said Karen.

January 18

I got cold feet at the airport. It was only days after the earthquake in Haiti. I was reeling with the global unimaginable tragedy of that one, and knew I was about to fly into the heart of another. So I called Bonnie. "Where is God in Haiti? Where will God be in the slums of Delhi?"

She said that in Haiti, as a result of the devastation, we've seen the care with which people treat people in trouble, with which we attend to our families and others, in chaos or sorrow. And I would get to see that in India.

She said, "Dearest, remember? You are going to India to see the holy sites, the holy tree, the holy marigolds, the whole holy enchilada, as someone once put it: the light that is divine.

"It will be beyond anything you've gotten to see before, and yet deeply recognizable. You are going to see whatever you expect to see. The only control you have is to plan your intention. You can go there to see God from another perspective, like seeing Mount Tam from San Quentin instead of Mill Valley. The experience of being in this form, human life, is always that we are born, live however long, die — this is true in deep poverty and great wealth. You can see God in the extreme disease and deformation, because the disease and the deformation of each person is not who that person is. Think Mother Teresa: in every person and each ravaged body, she saw the face of Jesus, both Christ crucified and the radiant face of God. Go see grace everywhere, passion, tenderness, art, families, surprise, mystery."

"But what if my plane crashes, or a snake bites me, or I catch a deadly disease, and I never get to see Sam and Jax again?"

"Well, good news," Bonnie said. "Life is eternal. Go see eternity."

January 20
I arrived in a socked-in Delhi at two a.m. I

156

was met by a cabbie sent by my hotel, who drove me through the fog like Mr. Toad, hell-bent and blind. I was in bed at four, and up before nine, when I was to meet Bill Hanson, who had been in India for two weeks already, at a Buddhist retreat with his teacher. I felt strangely okay, having been on a widely discredited anti–jet lag diet for four days. The hotel was small, tucked away from the main street, with marble floors, and no shower in my small bathroom, just faucets extending over the tile floor, so that you sat on a plastic stool like some washed-up old tribal chief, sploshed room-temperature water all over yourself, sudsed up, and rinsed off. There was a pair of men's worn flip-flops, which at first I recoiled from, and then ended up using frequently.

I went to Bill's room to begin our day, and knocked on the door.

He peered at me from around the door. "I'm naked," he announced, and pointed me to the hotel dining room.

Bill Hanson is Bill and Emmy Smith's oldest friend from the East Coast. He's close to seventy, a former Peace Corps teacher and manager, and he speaks a dozen languages. He is handsome, fussy, Buddhist, with blue eyes and a monk's tonsure. He has a piercing knowledge about most places on earth. The first time I met him, twenty years ago, I thought to myself, Paul Lynde, someone who managed to be both masculine and feminine, and who makes a joke out of everything, and is swishy in a nonspecific way.

When we stepped out of the hotel, Bill told me that if I gave a single rupee to a single beggar, he would leave me there in the dirt and dust of Old Delhi to fend for myself.

India looks like every movie I've ever seen of India, the way Georgia O'Keeffe always looked exactly like herself. People were going about their day: Brahmans, vendors, beggars, rickshaw drivers, schoolchildren in eentsy-beentsy buses. Some people were waking up under blankets: families who lived on the streets in this soft fever dream, with temporary homes built against low walls and fences. A kitchen materializes when the mother produces two bricks and some dung and someone has found pieces of coal or wood from packing crates; they have a rice pot and a minimal amount of grains to cook. In the market stalls were great vats of milk boiling, and clay pots in which yogurt would be made, from warm milk and yesterday's curds. Everywhere, people were doing their daily *puja,* their offering of flowers, fruit, devotions: in their stalls, on their blankets, in their rickshaws, in their fleeting homes on the street.

Bill waved away every beggar by saying, "Nay! Nay!" and it was painful for me, as I seriously wanted to start saving everyone, with a few rupees and some of the nice granola I had in my purse. But Bill gave me the stink-eye. "I will leave you here," he reiterated, and I remembered that when I first got sober, someone told me to take the action, and the insight would follow, and that when all else failed, follow instructions. So I committed to saying no to everyone: Nay, nay! It's all corruption, Bill explained, it's *Oliver Twist*: you don't give the beggars money, because it doesn't go to them — it goes to each beggar's *goonda,* the Fagin character, the thug who runs the beggar syndicate.

There are monkeys on the roofs and in the crazy canopy of the absolutely unfathomable spaghetti tangle of electrical wires, bizarrely shoved and hanging and twisted, which is your basic Indian electricity delivery system.

There are a million betel-leaf sellers on the streets, with their rolls of bright packets like condoms. There are teeny stalls packed together like timber, barely wider than a person's body, from which are sold all manner of things. Ultra-poor Muslims huddle in front of restaurants where they are fed real food, not leftovers, for free. All of life is being lived right here, every generation and social standing in a crowded parade. It is not a place where people get on the subway and go home. Life is lived lower to the ground: mothers and grandmothers holding babies go into squat to rest, or reconnoiter, or pee, and rise with grace, their babies still attached. The babies and children have mastered the cling here. I saw a few mothers holding out infants to pee and even on one occasion poop — diapers are not so common here. They are used for backup, if at all: mothers learn to read their babies' gestures, to predict every sound, fidget, reflexive move that might indicate impending elimination. Maybe I will not mention this to Amy.

I would imagine there is less fixation here on the baby's life of the mind than there is back in Marin. I bet not many of these Indian babies have the black-and-white mobiles provided to newborns at baby showers all over the United States to boost their spatial reasoning.

There are goats in ski parkas and sweaters milling around, tended by boys who want ten rupees from tourists to take a photograph of them and their goats. Bill says no, that this will count against me, but he stops to chat with them in his most animated Paul Lynde way. There are sadhus everywhere, wandering holy men wrapped in ragged warm blankets, sitting before tiny fires, smiling from deep within. The smells of spices, incense, humanity, cooking, marijuana hang in the air.

We got into an auto-rickshaw. Bill bargained Driver-ji down, while I wanted to pay him way more than he asked, plus give him my socks and shawl. Bill talked to the driver in Hindi, and then indicated me with a wave and a flourish:

"This is my former wife," he said in English, "and we are on our friendship tour." This turned out to be his major coping strategy in India. Everywhere we went, he bantered with drivers, waiters, beggars, almost always sharing some miserable aspect of our imaginary marriage: that I was cheap, or wouldn't put out, or had taken him to the cleaners when we broke up. And I laughed every time, so I guess it was my coping strategy, too.

There is no way to prepare for the mystical *zap* that is India. It's stunning, tragic, hallucinatory, bejeweled, smoky, overpowering. I've noticed that many people here have tiny hygiene issues. My automatic response to overwhelming situations is to try to organize everyone into small functioning groups. This usually requires a clipboard and Post-its. But these were hard to find in India. And the people did not seem to want me to organize them and improve their lot. They, and India, are the song that never ends, no matter what has been thrown at them over the millennia, or earlier this morning. You see packs of children begging, whose parents often put them up to this (another reason Bill won't let me give them money, as it encourages them not to pursue a real trade); minuscule open-air buses full of Muslim children in uniforms heading to school; packs of young glue-sniffing teenagers, zoned out. The smell of pot is everywhere.

Bill tells me that in Nepal, there is a phrase, *rungi-chungi jilli-milli,* which means total bombardment on every level, too much of everything all at once. Every color, smell, taste, sound, and echo fills the air, hot and spicy curries, every kind of sweet, harmony and silence and horns honking.

The air here is as soft as cashmere. Saris are for sale everywhere, and most women, no matter how poor, are works of art. There are way more men on the street than women — Bill says all the Muslim women are home, behind walls.

Most of the women I do see are petite, with long black hair and round brown eyes. My eyes played tricks on me, and I saw Amy everywhere in a sari.

I almost backed into a bull on the street while I gaped at a crowd of *hijra*s, whom you see all over: they are men in body only, who adopt female gender identity; they're not quite transvestites, and not transgendered. Some have castration surgery, some do not. There is no equivalent word or adequate definition in English. You cannot believe that some of them were born men. They are low-status, marginalized, and are often sex workers. Others look like male movie stars in saris. People are afraid of them, as they are always crashing ceremonies to which they have not been invited. You pay them to go away when they hit on you for money, or you risk their putting dark spells on you and yours. *Hijra*s frequently stand outside the homes of families with newborns until they are paid not to put curses on the children.

The horns of the bull that almost gored me were painted with the colors of the Indian flag, green, orange, white. The bull pulled a cart with sacks of rice. I stepped aside at the last minute, like a matador. Ubiquitous urchins laughed at me, and I smiled.

India is a round place: round noses and round, soulful eyes; sacks of grain; beach balls for sale everywhere; kids with hacky sacks; fried balls of anything edible for sale, savory or sweet.

It is layers upon layers of ancient and living civilization, a profound and tangible sacredness that has been alive for 7,000 years, always and still evolving, so maybe not exactly the song that never ends, but more like a song that has no beginning and no end, a Möbius-strip song, the same ancient note that ever was. Delhi is built upon and built upon and built upon the most ancient foundation, the Stone Age; the Indus Valley civilization from more than 5,000 years ago, the birth of most great religions; the Mughal empire; the sadhus, the yogis, and the British. The obscene Raj takeover left gorgeous buildings and squares and gardens everywhere. Everything is right there on the streets — everything that ever was, everything beautiful and destitute that ever was and will be, with Stone Age fires along the streets burning outside high-tech corporate offices, the Divine being transmitted and worshipped, and the reality and the continuity of that; and the dirt and pee and people shitting in the streets, and a million beggars right around you, and two million dogs, and as many cows and bulls, and every God everywhere, so that this sense of worship envelops everything, permeates and emanates. Other places I've seen in Asia, Thailand and Vietnam, for instance, seem as though they are behind glass, whereas here, you're a part of it. In Thailand, it's a great ballet or a play — a representation. But here I was part of it, part of the dance.

What people are faced with is mind-blowing, yet everywhere you see people getting up, making their fires, the women stirring, the men shaving, getting the kids clean and combed, ready for school; just getting on with things, in a much better mood than I would be in.

The wooden tables at the yogurt stalls are stacked with clay bowls that will be used only once, and never again, because meat-eating lips may have touched them. You're rotten and polluted if you're not a Brahman. The business class does not want to share even a well-washed bowl with disgusting putrefied old you.

The ordinary poor people are fourth-caste. Even lower, people who sweep, deal with bodies and shit, or work with leather are the Non-Scheduleds.

I, sweet adorable me, would not be allowed to step over the threshold of a Brahman's house.

Bill continued to tell anyone who spoke even rudimentary English that I was his ex-wife, and about our friendship tour, and said not to offer me any alcoholic beverages, as I would end up back in the gutters. Also, not to lend me money. "I am afraid I found this out the hard way," he grimly told the man at the coffee stall, who nodded politely. I couldn't help laughing. Without his constant patter, I would have dissolved into a dust pile of grief.

The crush of extreme deprivation tears you apart. I said, "Nay, nay," harshly to the mothers who tugged on my sleeves, pleading, "Mama, Mama." And I said, "Nay, nay," to their babies who tugged on my sleeves with Jax-sized fingers, also saying, "Mama, Mama," in tiny Kewpie voices. Then, in a stroke of genius, I started adding "EnRaHa!" in a menacing tone. It is from the Mike Leigh movie *Happy-Go-Lucky,* in which a furiously tense driving instructor shouts "EnRaHa!" at the main character whenever she makes a mistake — he points to the side mirrors, and then the rearview, the all-seeing eye of Ra, and shouts "En-RaHa!" at her. Brake! Watch out! EnRaHa! So I waved each beggar away dismissively and shouted, "Nay, nay! EnRaHa!" all but batting people away; this was a side of me not so often seen, least of all by me. It *absolutely* threw or scared everyone off.

Life here became a lot easier after I turned on the beggars.

"Can't we give anyone any money?" I implored Bill later, at another coffee stall.

"You could start a riot. Beggars will end up being beaten after you create disturbance and panic. We're going to give it to people who can help," he pronounced. So we took money over to a friend of his who runs a foundation through which teachers go to the streets to teach girls to read.

There are scruffy, starving, mangy dogs everywhere, and you see people bring them plastic bags holding a little milk to drink.

Bill and I sat near the top stairs of the Jama Masjid, the great Red Mosque built by Shah Jahan, of Taj Mahal fame, to watch life on the streets. They spread forth like crazy roiling runners woven of people. When the unearthly call to prayer sounded from a PA system only a few feet above us, like an air-raid siren or foghorn from antiquity, I leapt skittishly to my feet, like a cartoon cat, the whitest old lady in town.

On the way back to the hotel, Bill told our driver, "The ex wants to give all the money to beggars, and bring all the dogs home. Now, there's one special bullock I've allowed her to keep. She's brought it to her room. The hotel room is packed with the sixteen children and the one bull. They are all watching the BBC and having snacks: Lay's potato chips and full-sugar Cokes." The driver nodded solemnly and said, "Coca-Cola," and so, Day One.

Thursday, January 21
The second day, Bill told the men at the front desk, "My former wife likes your dal very much. Don't you, darling? Every restaurant we go to, she orders dal. But yours? Yours she loves best." Dal is the ubiquitous lentil stew. It is one of my favorite foods here and a staple at home.

He told the man at the counter at a Jain bookstore that our marriage was "rocky" until the truth came out, that he was a major fruit.

He told each of our drivers about our divorce, plus the children and the bull whom I've brought to my room for chips, Cokes, and the BBC.

168

He is, everywhere he goes in the world, a trove of historical information, gleaned from travels and his extensive reading. He was here when Indira Gandhi was killed by two Sikh bodyguards in 1984, and saw the city devolve into smoke and riots. Floods of memories came back to him — his driver was Sikh, and people were trying to kill him. We spent several hours at the Indira Gandhi Memorial Museum, the white bungalow surrounded by trees and a magnificent garden that was her residence. Mohandas Gandhi, Mahatma, was the reason Bill first fell in love with India; he saw in Gandhi and in India the uniquely divine that he had been seeking in the West. He had seen Gandhi on TV and in magazines: the dhoti, the sandals, the spectacles, the cane, his spinning, his love, and his defeat of the British Empire with the goodness, simplicity, and faith of the Indians. Bill came here to see this for himself, and he has kept coming back.

We passed by the crystal pathway in the museum's garden, where Indira Gandhi was shot by her bodyguards. I sighed, and bowed my head to honor her.

India showed me reality: two concentric circles further from what life will usually show of itself, because India doesn't have the extra energy to work on the surface or appearance or veneer. So you see how animal, how human, how divine and bodily and mystical we are, and how this is all swirled together.

I was eating some of the best food of my life, as good as the great food of France. It was tandoori and Punjabi food. Punjabi is what we are used to in the States, but I was enjoying original versions, every family's greatest-hits versions. Food is usually served on *thalis* — plates with dividers to hold five or six kinds of food, with little condiment bowls around the edges for yogurt and bright hot sauces. You leave space in the middle for rice, and there are three kinds of bread, two kinds of dal, one sweet and one sour, plus a vegetable dish, my favorite being the crisp brown slices of cauliflower and blackened peppers. Chicken cooked in cinnamon, clove, paprika, and saffron; cardamom-flavored pudding, milk curd and semolina, which tastes somehow like delicious milky dish soap, the way cilantro tastes of deliciously soapy grass.

Babies were everywhere, part of the flowing saris, or peeking forth like baby kangaroos, eyes lined in kohl. I see Jax everywhere, his eyes framed only by those black, lush lashes. We took a rickshaw and a subway to

Humayun's monumental tomb, the first garden tomb of the Mughals. The sheer scale left me feeling thunderstruck and stupid: the ancient and imperial gardens, the great dome, the cupolas, arches, sarcophagi. I felt as though I might begin to stagger, Snaggletooth onstage doing Shakespeare. We wandered around for a couple of hours, and then went back to the hotel for naps. Bill told the bicycle rickshaw man, "Driver-ji, you see old white foreigners like me sometime? And they need to sleep in the afternoon? That's me: I need absolute dark and quiet for half an hour. My ex-wife has been *very* patient about this all these years."

The driver nodded eagerly, although he did not seem to speak English.

After naps, we walked through the streets for a few hours, to look in stalls, mosques, gardens. The babies and children here are gorgeous. Half of the little ones are so physically beautiful that they could work for the airlines. And the other half look like Ragu, like ticklish containers of the divine, sneaky little beings with secrets. I saw one toddler who looked exactly like an elephant's baby, yet managed also to be lovely. I stopped to flirt with him and his mother. You could almost feel the words that the baby wasn't saying out loud: "I could tell you the secret, but I don't need to, because you can see it everywhere if you simply look around and breathe." The mother tugged on my sleeve and said, "Mama," but Bill was glaring at me, so I just gave her half a muffin I had in my purse from breakfast.

The babies have shiny black hair, and eyes that you fall into like black pools or furry caves, like Jax's. He could pass here, except for those babyish diapers he insists on wearing.

We saw the original Mama beggar. She and the baby made a beeline for me. "Nay, nay!" I thundered, turning away. "EnRaHa."

"Why don't you bring them back to your hotel room?" Bill suggested. "Share your chips with them. Help them forget about their destitution."

He said the woman had a life, and was part of some community, and had people she returned to every night. Like the people who made a home on the street, where, in the early morning, someone would take a pot, and a match, and a piece of coal, and make a fire; the family would cook rice, and be together, and beg, and later in the afternoon, when, as Bill put it, they were off-duty, we'd see them maybe bathing at the public faucets.

172

I couldn't really tell if some people were dead or just sleeping. We approached an ancient prone man in a head wrap; he was so tiny, and lying so still in the dirt. I said to Bill, "Can I at least give that one money? I can't even tell if he's alive."

"Certainly not — you may not give that one money if he's dead. Honey, you have *got* to work on your boundaries."

Friday, January 22
We spent the morning walking around the sprawling, ancient, sinister but ethereal spice market: thousands of stalls and aromas, a riot of color and sparkle, and unbelievable squalor. Then to Jama Masjid, the biggest mosque in India — Bill has seen it many times, and so he sat outside on the steps to read William Dalrymple's great book on Delhi, *City of Djinns,* while waiting for me. I stepped into the courtyard of red sandstone. A gregarious man who looked to be my age came up, unasked, to act as my guide through the courtyard and the mosque. He gave me a loaner *hijab* to cover my loathsome female head, and I felt like Christiane Amanpour as he led me around the domes, towers, minarets; took a picture of me standing near the low tombs; and showed me the black-and-white-mosaic

173

workmanship of the great inside walls. The mosque leaves you flabbergasted. But when we turned to walk back to the entrance, he demanded money for the first time, two hundred rupees. I said a hundred, and he gave me a threatening look, but I bellowed, "EnRaHa!" at him and he backed off.

Most people were not wearing shoes. The pinkness of their palms and soles, when they sat resting, was quite striking and vulnerable, almost edible — the tops of their hands were as darkly rich as chocolate, and then underneath, you saw the universal pink.

I saw great, beautiful, difficult weirdness every inch of every street and alley. I was successfully still doing "EnRaHa" everywhere to chase away beggars. The begging and deformities were killing me, but Bill again maintained that it was useless to give money, because the beggars wouldn't get it. Yet they grabbed at you and knocked on taxi windows with their stumps and babies and leprosy, and cried to you in your rickshaw. I told them each firmly, "Nay, nay," then added, "EnRaHa," and looked away, so Bill wouldn't abandon me on the streets. I would hate to end up in some squalid jail even if it *had* been fashioned out of a formerly glorious Raj mansion.

I decided I would trap some monkeys later and start a Monkey Tea Party.

I would be the Chief Monkey.

Almost all the babies and little children I saw had kohl around their eyes — Bill said it was to protect them from the evil eye. I wondered if it had something in common with the eye black that football players wear around their eyes to protect them from the sun's fierce glare. I Googled "kohl on babies' eyes" on my tiny computer, and discovered that the lead in the powder from which kohl is made is toxic to the tiny flies that are everywhere in India; the kohl keeps the babies' eyes safe from fly infestation. I was worried sick about the effect of lead on children's eyes. Maybe I could form some consciousness-raising groups for the mothers.

We planned to go to bed early, as in the morning we were going to be driven to the airport for our flight to Varanasi. That evening our taxi driver drove us through a heavy San Francisco fog. There had been, and remained, a militaristic presence of wildly heightened security, cops everywhere for the last two days, and barricades going up. The formidable, sprawling Red Fort, built in the 1600s and capital of the Mughal empire until the mid-1800s, was closed

175

because the Republic Day parade would start there in a few days, and chaos was expected. We were in our rooms by nine. The sound of massive bombs exploding nearby sent me down to the front desk to inquire politely if we were under terrorist attack, but I was told it was only a wedding party. I put in my earplugs, and repeated *Baba nam kevalam* silently in my head until I eventually fell asleep.

Saturday, January 23

We were up early for our plane ride to Varanasi — the modern name for Benares — the holiest of cities, but before we left, the most fabulous thing happened. My Black-Berry rang, and it was Ragu calling from the ashram in Los Altos — he had arranged a conference call with me, and Sam and Amy, who were at my house, and Dada, who was at his orphanage in Delhi.

I thought I was dreaming at first, but decided to go with it.

"Hi, Mom," Sam said, and my heart swelled, but he was instantly cut off by Ragu, who shouted to Dada that "it is Anne, from Great Britain, who is so great! Remember?" Dada said something quietly in Hindi, and Ragu shouted back at him with enthusiasm, and then shouted for Sam to talk, so he said, "Hi, Mom," and then was interrupted again by Ragu. He wanted to explain how he had engineered this conference call, and how cheap it would be for him, and how maybe I could drop by Dada's orphanage while I was here, and then he shouted to Dada, "That is Anne! Sam's mother!" And then I heard Jax squawk, and I actually clutched at myself like Blanche DuBois, and Ragu then shouted for Amy to say hello, and as soon as she did, he interrupted her — he was like a crazy symphony conductor on acid. He made sure Dada was on the line. He was, but he seemed totally confused, and was speaking softly, possibly to himself, in Hindi. So Ragu talked to him loudly in English for a minute, and Dada spoke in Hindi and with obvious confusion, and an animated loud conversation ensued between the two of them. It was like a Marx Brothers comedy routine or an old radio show, like Bob and Ray, with no conversation going between me and Sam or Amy. But then I heard Jax babbling, and Amy said, "Jax, it's Nana!" But this, too, was interrupted by enormously loud vitality and excitement from Ragu. Then Sam said, "Mommy! Mommy! We are all fine, are you okay?" and I started to cry because I was so happy, so connected in this Mad Hatter symphony piece. I said I was the happiest I had ever been in my life, and Sam asked me to tell him a story, but then we were cut off as Ragu kept shouting to Dada that this was Anne, from Great Britain, who was so great and who wanted to come visit Dada at his orphanage, which I didn't quite remember having said. I surrendered and simply cried out every so often that I loved Sam and Amy and Jax, Ragu and Dada, and I cried out thanks over and over to Ragu for arranging our conference call. We were on the line for a little less than ten minutes, with perhaps a minute of direct "conversation" between me and Sam and Amy, and eight minutes of this Indian Who's on First, and Jax's squawks for a few seconds here and there, and I felt that this phone call was why I had come to India.

Because of the fog, almost no flights and no trains for Varanasi were leaving Saturday morning, and it was like being in the chill in the Outer Sunset district in August back home, but one plane — ours — eventually took off after a four-hour delay. We sat near a young Israeli beauty and her Lebanese boyfriend, who both spoke English, and whom Bill anointed as the Mideast's only remaining hope for lasting peace. They fell in love with him.

Varanasi was so *rungi-chungi-jilli-milli*-plus-plus that it made Old Delhi look organized; multilayered chaos and congestion and pandemonious beauty in the streets, with vendors, sadhus, rickshaw drivers, but mostly regular Indian families getting from one place to another. We checked into our hotels — I was staying at a nice one across the street from the river, Bill at a much cheaper one nearby (five dirt blocks away). We immediately headed for the Ganges, which was one block from my hotel, to the ghats of Benares. They make up a stone thoroughfare that runs along the river beneath the temples and mansions that rise like cliffs above the steps and sidewalk. Every kind of person you could ever imagine in India — monks and priests and devotees, hawkers, ragamuffins, food sellers — was there. Mark Twain famously said that Benares "is older than history, older than tradition, older even than legend, and looks twice as old as all of them put together." My hotel was at Assi Ghat, the southernmost end, and we walked along the huge stone steps that create the embankment of the Ganges, beneath the mansions built for royal family pilgrimages. Men of all ages bathed in the river, and drank from it, the very thought of which, as the old hymn puts it, caused me to tremble, tremble, tremble. Women and men did laundry, laying hotel sheets out to dry; people were talking or praying, rowing, selling, begging, feeding their children; cows, oxen, and horses milled in the sand. The younger holy men looked like they could be from Bolinas or Woodstock. Small fires burned everywhere, for every reason. The river was the color of mist.

Bill pointed way down the embankment to the burning ghat, where cremation takes place day and night, but I couldn't go there yet. I needed to eat and to get my bearings. You lose the known package of your nice organized self almost instantly here. Overeating is one way back, the way it is at funerals at home.

We went back to my hotel for dinner, but the dining room was too postmodern, too Louis Farouk, the ex–king of Egypt whose taste ran to deep red velvet drapes and chair upholstery, Las Vegas, Versailles, Elvis. I couldn't eat there. We walked through the crazy crowded street to Bill's hotel, with me shouting "EnRaHa!" at the beggars, and Bill laughing at how it always worked.

I collapsed at the dining room table. Bill ordered a beer with his dinner, but when the waiter arrived and began to fill my glass first, Bill said, "My ex is an alcoholic. She can't have any beer." The waiter brought me a sweet lime drink instead.

Sunday, January 24
We were on the Ganges at five in the morning, in a riverboat in the fog. One image that had called me to India for years, besides the Taj Mahal, was a dawn visit to the Ganges on a riverboat, for the sunrise.

All four mornings we were in Varanasi, our boat was socked in with fog. This morning's riverboat man said, "Too much the foggy!" which I think captures all of human life. It was a thick, white pea-soup fog — a vichyssoise fog — and apparently we were not going to see any of the sights I'd assumed we would see, and in fact had come here to see.

But we saw something else: We saw how much better mystery shows up in the fog, how much wilder and truer each holy moment is than any fantasy.

Through the cold vapor emerged outlines of buildings, and the palaces and water towers painted with images of gods, Shiva and Ganesh and Krishna, and boatfuls of other people who drifted by quietly, muted by the fog. What we saw was the river up close, because you couldn't see anything that was far away: gloriously, giddily colorful disinte-

181

grating figures of Saraswati, the goddess of learning, made of straw and clay, painted and adorned with flowers; the lights of fires on the distant shore; and candles on leaves floating a few feet away in the murky river.

I asked Bill if we should go back on land, wait for the sun to come out in a few hours, and then return.

"Oh, come on. It'll be fun," he replied. "We'll swirl around in the fog and watch the dead bodies float by."

It was so eerie. Spooky, in a strangely benevolent way. Annie Dillard said, "We awake, if ever we wake at all, to mystery." You believe, in India, that the unseen, the unfathomable, is the bedrock, that the unseeable is the truer reality, which doesn't work for me at all. I mean, I'm an American! I like to know where I am and what I am seeing and what it all means. On the other hand, I do like to shop. We bought trinkets from a rascal-eyed boatman who floated up beside our boat and then would not leave us alone. Bill lost patience. "Look," he told the man, "you've got your deal, we've got our deal. Now let's *all* move on to bigger and better things." The rascal-eyed boatman looked askance for a moment or two, then smiled and paddled away.

We saw people bathing in front of certain

ghats that are specific to their god. We saw
Brahmans instruct — i.e., shove — their
reluctant sons and nephews into the freez-
ing dirty water, and dozens of formerly
fantastic, now deteriorating floating Saras-
watis from a festival honoring her two days
before. Of course they disintegrate, as we
all do. They would be taken away by the
river, into the Unseen, like the bodies we
saw being cremated, becoming smoke and
then merging with the fog.

Back on land, we walked for hours, and
then went to our hotel rooms for naps.

Nothing could ever seem as gorgeous and
bizarre as what I had seen that day; until
my BlackBerry pinged, to indicate a text,
from Sam:

"Come home, Mom! Jax can now do the
pre-crawl, kind of scooch across the floor.
Also, he can almost read, I swear to God.
Or at least hold a book now for twenty
seconds or so, like he's reading it. Then he
starts trying from various directions to eat
it."

I met up with Bill at sunset. He was sitting on the steps of Assi Ghat, flirting with
an Indian family. He threw himself into my
arms with extravagant relief when I walked
up. "This is *her*," he told them, and they
clapped. "I told them, I can't find my ex-

wife. And they tried, with no success, to comfort me." Bill and I walked down the ghats and joined a group of people gathered around a man with a small monkey. The man asked me if I wanted to pet it, so I did, and as I turned away, it leapt onto my head. I could have been killed, conceivably! But it was so hilarious, and the couple of dozen Indians watching laughed in a very loving way. Everyone loves my dreads. The monkey played with them. Then he got his hands tangled up in them and tried to jump away, and almost succeeded, but the guy put him back on me because we had drawn a crowd, and therefore profit. When the man finally tried to unhook him, the monkey scratched my hand.

Instantly, all I could think of was Dustin Hoffman in *Outbreak* — the Ebola-infected pet monkey spreading it to Americans. And me without my Purell, which was back in my room, and is very effective against hemorrhagic viruses.

I went to the front desk of my hotel to ask if the person on duty had any emergency disinfectant, and the manager told me to go downstairs and see the hotel nurse. I found a beautiful Bollywood woman in nurse clothes, sitting with her Bollywood boyfriend, and I explained about the monkey attack and showed her my small scratch and asked for antiseptic or antibiotic ointment to prevent Ebola or Marburg.

Unfortunately, she did not speak English.

But the boyfriend spoke a little, and became our translator. I asked for Purell, demonstrating how calm and grown-up Americans could be. The boyfriend translated, but the nurse told him, No Purell. I rubbed my hands faster, to indicate dire urgency. She shook her head. I asked for rubbing alcohol. Nay, nay — no rubbing alcohol. Fine, I said sort of huffily, "Fine, let me use your soap and hot water." Oh dear, no soap or hot water at the nurse's station.

Now I was extremely frustrated, as the virus coursed through my veins, and I was about to stomp off when the boyfriend said, "Wait! We have a veddy excellent cream!" He went into the secret nurse chamber and returned with a tube that said "anti-fungal" on the label. Veddy excellent, he assured me, and gave me a dab in a water bottle cap. I stared at it for a moment. I smiled, thanked them, and headed up to my room to use my own Purell, and then the anti-fungal cream.

The next day we ate our meals at the restaurant at Bill's hotel, and then went to find our permanent boatmen, Ashok and Max. Ashok was delicate as a deer, Max much more Western, like Gomez Addams. Every so often Ashok would throw a handful of crispy dough bits from a bag into the water beside our boat, and the seagulls would descend screaming in a cloud to pick them off the river, inches from the boat. We walked among Brahmans and beggars of every age, and people selling food, and *batti.* This means "light" — the little flower boats with candles that you light for devotion and float on the Ganges. The Flower Boat Children descended on us like mosquitoes, and I EnRaHa'ed them all, except when Bill was distracted, in which case I furtively bought their *batti.* "Uncle, Uncle," they beseeched him, and he waved them away, except for a persistent little boy in a Spider-Man T-shirt, whom even Bill could not resist. People carried bodies wrapped in cloth on litters, Papaji or Mamaji covered with flowers, and headed to the fires, headed to the river. Bodies burn all day and night. You stop even noticing.

We knew a few people after a while — the nurse, the nurse's boyfriend, Ashok and

Max. Bill came upon the Israeli woman and her Lebanese boyfriend who had sat near us on the plane. We stood around together at the burning ghat. Bill asked the young Lebanese man if he read much, and he said yes, and Bill pleaded with him to buy all my books. Bill said that I was down on my luck and that he'd had to lend me money, but now he could see that there was no chance of getting it back. Plus, he added, he was too embarrassed to ask me for it. They commiserated with him. I smiled sheepishly. We all hugged and kissed good-bye, our eyes burning from the smoke of the bodies on the nearby pyres.

That night on our way to find Max and Ashok, I casually dismissed a boy who was trying to sell me *batti,* and near tears he cried out, "Auntie," and ripped open his outer shirt. "I'm Spider-Man!" And indeed he was, the one Bill had not been able to resist. I splurged on his *batti.*

Tomorrow night Bill and I fly back to Delhi, and then Wednesday I take a car ride to Agra for the Taj. So two and a half more full days in India.

We took our nightly riverboat ride past the burning ghat to the evening prayer ritual, which involves Brahman priests and so much fire and incense and displays of

187

light that it makes Catholic High Mass look like a Mennonite service. At least a thousand people were gathered at this ghat, reverential and pumped, carrying torches and candles, and it made me think of the Tribal Council on *Survivor*. But then, it was also hypnotic and lovely, with the Ganges, mist, and the boats and white sand of the far shore across the river as a backdrop. Tonight a holy man came up to me and made a red powder *bindi* on my forehead with his thumb, like red Ash Wednesday ashes. When I got back to my hotel room, I went to wash and nearly cried out when I saw it, because I'd already forgotten it was there; my first thought when I saw myself in the mirror was that I was bleeding out from monkey Ebola.

By that time my scratch was slightly red and puffy; pre-hemorrhagic. I used lots of Purell and antifungal cream, prayed furiously, read the great novel of India, *Shantaram,* for hours, and slept well, and this morning most of the puffy redness was gone. It was a medical miracle.

Tuesday, January 26
Today was abridged; we were going to leave for Delhi at three. In the morning I walked alone along the Ganges, watched the mist rising, people doing their laundry on the

rocks by the river, washermen and washer-
women laying out hotel sheets to dry. I
passed the monkey man with the monkey
on his shoulder and gave him a big thumbs-
up.

It was International Annie Defies Bill and
Gives Away Money to the Beggars Day. I
gave an old beggar granny with big feet my
Birkenstocks, and my socks that had a festive moose print. I wondered what she made
of them. I gave a begging mother my long-
sleeved Gap T-shirt; next time I will pack
only things I can leave behind. After I
checked out of the hotel, I stood outside
with my carry-on and forty ten-rupee notes
(each worth about a quarter). I went to the
ghat in front of the hotel. There were two
nice, manageable beggar moms with little
babies on the steps, all four crying to me,
"Mama, Mama," and pantomiming feeding
themselves with a fork. I whipped out my
tens, and gave one to the first mom, and
one to the second, and then one to a third
who had appeared, and then another to a
grabby sadhu; and suddenly it was like
when the seagulls roared in a cloud straight
at us on Ashok's boat. Dozens of beggars
descended on me, calling, "Mama, Mama,"
and "Auntie, Auntie." I was handing out
ten-rupee notes to all these hands that were

tearing and snatching at me — and I was scared to fucking death. I felt like Tippi Hedren in *The Birds*. I was shouting, "Nay! Nay! EnRaHa! EnRaHa!" but boy, talk about closing the barn door after the horses get out. There were easily forty or fifty beggars surrounding terrorized, white, cringy me, and then some sort of security person from my hotel pushed into the crowd and starting shoving the mommies and babies and miscellaneous beggars away and rebuking them all, and another security man in a cap arrived, swinging at them with a stick, and he pulled me out of the vortex. I broke free and fell down, but caught myself. I sat down on the ground trying to catch my breath. I felt like a chick that had pecked its way out of its shell, lying there in the wet plop of freedom, with security making batting motions at beggars and with the curious peering at me on my butt.

When I met up with Bill at his hotel and told him what had happened, he cried out with distress. Then he flamboyantly zipped his mouth closed to avoid saying he had told me so, but he sniggered off and on all the way to the airport.

Wednesday, January 27
I woke up early in Delhi, and had a big

breakfast in my room, a cheese omelet, several pieces of wheat toast, and an orange. I tapped on the door of Bill's room down the hall to say good-bye, but he didn't answer. I went outside and stood waiting for my driver to Agra, game for a total immersion in quintessential India.

Then an e-mail from Sam arrived on my BlackBerry:

"We are so excited you are coming home. I know we told you that Jax is pre-crawling, which might make you think he is up on all fours — but that is not exactly true. What he can do is the army crawl, using his elbows for rapid propulsion across the floor, with occasional success at getting on his knees. So don't be disappointed. It is great anyway! Come home!"

I hit the lottery with my driver, Prem. He spoke English, sort of, and pronounced Bush's name Jaja W. Boot, which made the entire trip worth it. He drove the car you see everywhere in India, an Ambassador, which looks like a small, fat Peugeot with a snub-nosed hood. Bill had told me that its marketing slogan used to be "The King of Indian Roads." Most of the Ambassadors are old, and either black, as they were originally in the 1940s, or white, from when they became official government cars.

Prem and I talked about our children and shared my roast cashews and a large chocolate bar. I was glad to leave the city and be in the Indian countryside, passing fields and the suggestions of villages, lots of animals. Everything was fine — except that our car started breaking down. It broke down four times in the first four hours after we left Delhi.

Each time, Prem assured me that it would take just a second to repair, that it was just loose wires. I pretended not to be worried sick. The car broke down by the side of the road in the countryside, and once alongside a curb in a town where beggars descended on it. I made a gesture of waving them away, looking with great annoyance to the opposite window, where there were another dozen beggars. One man on a cart who had leprosy tapped on the window the entire time, smiling.

Finally, I rolled the window down to just above the highest his arm stumps could reach, and said, very nicely, with Christian love, "Nay, nay. EnRaHa!"

The third time the King broke down, when Prem appeared from beneath the hood with his tools, he asked if I knew anything about car wiring. Me. I can just barely work a toaster.

I said, "Jeez, no, not really." He went back under the hood with a strip of cloth, came out, and then got the car running. We started up again, and were soon passing fields full of beans and grain and rice, and every so often fourth-world outdoor cafés with white plastic lawn chairs. I laughed out loud at the memory of Father Guido Sarducci saying, "Where did the lawn chairs come from? And what do they want?" Prem and I talked off and on in our best broken efforts about our children, the glue-sniffing children on the streets of Delhi, Obama, and Jaja W. Boot. We were quiet for long stretches. It was an honor to see the countryside with him.

After several hours, much longer than I had expected it would take, we got to the gates of the Taj Mahal. Prem turned me over to his cousin, who worked as a guide there, who spoke perfect English and had a name made up of dozens of syllables.

I had wondered often since we'd set out this morning if it was really worth the time and effort to come here on my last full day in India. I had seen the image of the Taj Mahal a thousand times, and I'd thought I was prepared, but I couldn't possibly have been, any more than I was for the Great

193

Sphinx at Giza, or Jax. The Taj Mahal fills you with such awe that you feel stoned. The great spotless-white rising domed marble mausoleum, the four minarets, the garden; it's perfection. It is beauty; it is truth.

Prem's cousin and I walked solemnly around the grounds for a couple of hours. He told me the history of the Mughal empire and about Shah Jahan and his grief when his wife died. I told him about Jax and Sam. He pointed out the most unbelievable details, mostly inside the mausoleum, where the walls are inlaid with millions of bits of jigsawed gemstones — sapphire, carnelian, lapis, turquoise, coral, topaz. Its sheer glory stupefied me, like a lightning strike in slow motion. I got out my pictures of Jax, and the dogs.

The Taj made me laugh out loud, because it is so amazing, and I cried because I was here for only this one time. Prem's cousin gave me his handkerchief. Dabbing at my eyes, I asked him to tell me his name again. It was Rasoolasallahualayi-wassallam, or something. I asked if I could call him "Cousin," and he smiled and said yes.

Cousin handed me back to Prem, and we headed back to Delhi. We drove maybe fifteen minutes before the car started acting up. Prem tore a bleached-out red mechanic's rag into strips, and disappeared under the hood again. Then I had an inspiration. I tore out the blue cord handle from a bag I had. The cord was pretty thick, almost a foot long. The next time the car failed, about fifteen minutes later, Prem started to get out of the car; I dangled the blue cord toward him, and the relief on his face was radiant.

Thursday, January 28
Bill had promised that we would walk to all of our pet places in Delhi today, maybe take a subway ride. I was flying home at night. We went back to my favorite restaurant for one last *thali* lunch, six dishes on the divided metal plate, two kinds of chapatis. We went to see the Red Fort, finally, the great fortress of gates, courtyards, a moat, and breathtaking mausoleums, and then visited some storefront temples whose walls were decorated in mosaics that seemed to have been created out of peacock feathers, meadows, candle flame, each temple worthy of a day's attentions. But all I really wanted to do was marinate one last time in the street life.

A gorgeous, sexy woman vendor said sweetly to Bill, "Banana?" He shook his head and we kept walking. She called to him again, more seductively, almost suggestively,

"Banana?" He smiled. Then, as we walked past, she screamed at the top of her lungs, "BANANA?"

Bill admitted, after nine days, that there was one person in all of India he felt bad about not giving money to, a woman who had been begging at the subway entrance for a starving guy who lay on the ground beside her, who Bill had heard was dying of AIDS. So, a few hours before I went to the airport, we came upon them on the stairs to the subway. This guy looked much worse than Bill had described — as if he'd been exhumed and cleaned up, though not particularly well. He weighed maybe sixty pounds, and had the hands of death, badly receded teeth, biblical dirtiness, wild eyes.

Bill approached them and dropped coins into their cup, and I put in most of the bills I had left. I said to them both, "Bless you, bless you," over and over, beseeched them with my eyes. I was kind of unhinged on their behalf. Then I had to walk on, because of the crush behind me.

A beautiful young woman with two pretty female companions fell in step with me and tugged my sleeve.

"Oh my God — you must *never* give anything to those two."

I looked over at her and her two companions, who rolled their eyes.

Bill said, "But he's obviously about to die."

"Oh, no," said one of the young women. "Those two have been there forever. He stays in that condition so his wife can beg off him."

Shocked, I said, "That can't be." But all three young women nodded. Bill and I instantly got that we'd been had but good: we were so busted. We laughed and for a while talked about beggars with the three women, who were university students.

"What about the starving little kids?" I asked. "Don't you help them?"

"No, no," one of the women said adamantly. "If they are successful at begging, it just makes them want to keep doing it. They'll never learn a trade."

"But how do these children eat otherwise?"

"They will probably go home for dinner. Their parents will feed them. Their parents are the ones who put them up to this."

Bill and I laughed at ourselves all the way to our train, helpless as little kids.

I still sort of thought that we should notify someone from the All India Institute of Medical Sciences, and maybe get the guy at the subway a checkup. But for once I could not inflict my goodness and good ideas on the world, because I had to get back to the hotel and pack.

Sunday, January 31
I don't really remember much about flying home, except that it took several years and was pretty awful and that I did the best I could. I rode a cab home from the airport, and now I have been here for two days, and have seen Jax, Amy, and Sam. My house now seems like a bungalow in Beverly Hills, so quiet and clean, with beautiful rugs and fixtures everywhere, and running water in three out of six rooms.

Jax is six months old, and will not need us for much longer. He is a fully formed person with a nice tan and huge black eyes, who now rolls over, and over, and over. I keep thinking of Teri Garr as Inga in *Young Frankenstein*, having a roll in the hay cart, crying out joyfully, roll, roll, roll. Jax is happy and social, rocks and kicks and rolls. He bounces when you hold him in a standing position, and sits, briefly, before falling over like a drunk.

Amy and Sam seemed to be in a good place when I got back, but demented with jet lag, I had to grip myself by the wrist not to pitch one good idea after another at them. I didn't say, "Let's find some great day care for Jax, so Amy can *work* part-time," but I writhed with the effort to stay silent. I almost offered to babysit twice a week to this end, but didn't. Since Jax's birth, my ideas about what would be best for everyone usually got in the way. Life is already an obstacle course, and when you're adding your own impediments (thinking they're helping), you really crazy it up. You make it harder to even just cross the room. You should not *bring* more items and hurdles to the obstacle course.

February 2

It was pouring rain when I woke. I drove up in the storm to see Millard today. The end is near. He was restless and jerky, in Beckett agitation, like the lady onstage rummaging through her bag. But this discomfort and squirm may launch him into what awaits.

He was a total exaggeration of how this life does not work — he urgently needed to do his lists, and make phone calls, and all this felt frantically imperative to him. I'm really seeing how the machine of our lives is always on the fritz, whether because of our bodies' failing us, or our minds'. Millard's twitchy end-stage agitation looks the way a lot of us feel sometimes, even if we seem fine on the outside.

For some reason, my cousins did not call in hospice while I was in India. It was driving me crazy. I want to make lists of what they need to do, and make their calls for them. But all I can do is show up, laugh with Millard, listen, and breathe with him. All I can do is sit and bring my love to him.

During a moment when he was quieted, like a horse, he told me he was worried that he would live too long like this. I told him about the end of my father's days, the flurry before the final deep sleep, and how peacefully he passed.

The rainstorm was grotesquely elemental, sheets of blowing rain, a nightmare on the roads. Someone was playing with the hose up there!

I don't think it's a coincidence that Millard waited for me to get home from India, or that I was in such a jet-lagged mess. The supposed succor of the familiar world, which I missed in India, was not going to bolster me. And it was not going to give comfort to Millard, either — there was not much relief for him, on this side.

I had no choice but to feed the animals, walk the dogs, get my work done, help take care of Jax, talk to friends, and be in what was true. It's always the same old problem:

how to find our*selves* in the great yammer-
ing of ego and tragedy and discomfort and
obsession with everyone else's destinies.

February 3
I miss India, in a way. I had fewer problems
to solve there. Actually, I hardly had any,
except when I got the monkey tangled in
my hair. Oh, and the riot I started in Varanasi. India was spectacular and difficult,
timeless, immediate, and demanding —
mood-altering, with its ecstatic overwhelm
and horror and beauty. I really had to pay
attention.

Here at home, I had a different set of
problems. Millard rapidly deteriorating.
Amy not working. And the dogs have ticks,
and the ticks might bite Jax and give him
Lyme disease and a lifetime of physical and
psychiatric problems. I felt crazy, sad, helpless, like everything was coming together by
coming apart. It's good to be reminded of
the fraying weave of the world, but not with
advanced jet lag. It is the most difficult Zen
practice to leave people to their destiny,
even though it's painful — just loving them,
and breathing with them, and distracting
them in a sweet way, and laughing with
them.

Whose life was I living? I was living Annie's life (and maybe a bit of the dogs'). And it was complex enough. I had enough to wrestle, wrangle, and settle back into, with this one life of mine. Besides, I knew beyond a shadow of doubt that if something was not my problem, I probably did not have the solution.

There are no words for how much I hate, resent, and resist this.

February 5
The bucketing rain stopped. Amy called to say she and Jax were coming over later, and inwardly I felt like Lily and Bodhi when I get out the cheese treats, unable to focus on anything else, all but panting. This is terrible.

I went up to see Millard for an hour. He looked like some skinny old prophet from Leviticus at a computer. He was alternately agitated, frantic, in love with me, taking pills randomly, lucid, the man he always was, and nuts. He was sitting elegantly in his chair, telling me how much he had to do; then he suddenly leapt up, looking fearful and angry, his teeth gritted, and sprayed us both with a can of lemony air freshener — as if giant insects were dive-bombing us, and he was going to save us from attack. The air reeked.

202

Then he sat down, phoned someone, and said calmly, "Linda, I have to cancel the presentation for March fourth. I'm comfortable, but in no position to present anything now — least of all myself. . . . No, I do not expect to be any better. In fact, a great deal worse. And that's okay with me."

He weighed at least ten pounds less than when I had left for India, and while his mind was funky, he was distinctly himself. He said that he was ready to go home and see my aunt Pat, and that he would give my love to my mother, Pat's twin, and to my father. He has always assured me that modern physics can prove that the soul survives death. My house is filled with books by scientists that he has foisted on me over the years — my dumb, blind, unscientific faith has always driven him crazy. Even today, he tried to pick a small fight about my lamb-to-the-slaughter beliefs, then kindly insisted that his beloved physics can prove the survival of the soul. Of course, he had been gobbling down Oxycontin, so that may have had something to do with it.

February 7
Sam, Amy, and Jax came for a visit, during which Sam and Amy did many loads of

laundry and in all possible ways took advantage of my generous nature, but they left me with Jax while they stole off to take naps. I have become a pathetic old junkie, stoned with delight. Jax alternately jumped up and down on my leg as if he were in a Johnny Jump Up, and quietly explored the world: my eyes, nostrils, dreads, and Mary medallion, Lily's ears, the kitty's tail, which whipped back and forth above us from the top of the couch, like Indiana Jones's whip. Then I gave him a bottle, and held it for him, although technically he could hold it by himself.

I told him, "I don't know what is going to happen to you, and what your life will be like, but this is not in my hands. You have your own higher power." He took this in gravely. Sam padded in from his nap and began chattering away instantly with Jax, and snatched him away from me with gentle father hands.

Hmmph. I watched Sam and Jax gaze at each other while Jax sucked on the bottle. To have mothered this young father fills me with visceral feelings of awe, joy, and dread. Love, fierce pride, a new power, and faint anxiety flitted across Sam's face: you love your kids way too much to ever feel safe again. I could see in his love that this baby had broken his turtle shell, the way Sam broke mine.

February 9

I got up early and went for a walk in the drizzle with the dogs and my friend Karen. We laughed our way along the trail behind the dogs: heaven. Then I went to see Millard, not knowing if he would be alive. He was, but even closer to death, wheezing more, yet his mind was sharp when he woke from his nap. Mozart's Concerto for Flute and Harp wafted from his CD player. We talked about my father's death, what a great way to go it was — morphine and music, your kids there to lean down and kiss you on the head and neck. My cousin Ricky came in to do that more than once when I was at Millard's, as my brothers had done with Dad thirty years ago.

Millard was not quite to the end zone, not *quite* ready to spike the ball and do the chicken dance. But I wondered whether I'd see him again on this side.

After I got home, Amy and Jax, Stevo and Clara arrived for the afternoon. Stevo calls Jax "Manolito." Clara calls him "Cuz," and struggles to hold him now that he has become a wiggly bouncing sack of potatoes. It was easier when he was the size of a dinner loaf and moved only his hands and legs.

Now there are things he wants, *now,* and he fusses if denied. If you ask me, babies are already ruined by seven months old. Once you drive them off the lot, they lose fifty percent of the Blue Book value. Poor little guy, having to be here. I said to Karen that you're instantly in a bind once you arrive here on earth, of need, self-will, a body and a separate personality, even before the crippling self-consciousness kicks in, even before seventh grade. Rashes, instinct, and cravings for the bottle, the breast. (Karen said that this would be a great name for a pub — The Bottle and Breast.)

She said that you're fucked at cell division, that it's all downhill from there. After that, it's all survival, and trying to keep yourself either entertained or convinced that the things you're obsessed with are of any importance at all in the big scheme.

February 10

My cousin Ricky left a message at five in the morning that Millard had died peacefully in his sleep. I went up to see his daughter, my cousin Kathy, at their house. She met me at the front door, stout and buxom and gorgeous, with short black curls and a movie-star mouth; she is five years younger than I. Millard's body had already been taken away. I knew they would not be sitting shiva — Millard had once said they were bagelly Jews — but I'd wanted to see his body, because seeing the body has always helped me say good-bye to loved ones.

Kathy came to the door eating a huge Dagwood sandwich. I said, "Are you okay, baby?" and she said, "I'm in the cold-cuts stage of grief."

I wrote an obituary for our local paper on Millard's computer. Kathy dug out all the relevant dates. He was born in San Francisco in 1923, a few months after my dad; he went to San Francisco State and got an advanced degree from UC Berkeley in history. He married his great love, my aunt Pat, my mom's twin, in 1949 after serving in World War II on Graves Detail, which involved engineering cemeteries for the war dead. This immersion in mortality gave him a deep appreciation for beauty and life and great food. He loved his friends, and hiking, and Julia Child, who was always the other woman in his marriage. He pursued a profound lifelong study of history, physics, faith, and the recipe for the perfect cassoulet. He taught at the College of Marin for three decades. He had four children, Robby,

Ricky, Kathy, and the youngest, David, three grandchildren, two living nephews (two had died), two nieces, two great-nephews, a great-niece, and one great-great-nephew, now almost seven months old.

February 14
I gave Sam and Amy tickets to an early movie and the promise of a home-cooked dinner for Valentine's Day, and when they walked off into town, I took Jax to the park. We sat on a bench at the redwood grove with a sweet local guitar player. He played my favorite Beatles song, "In My Life," and then Carole King's "You've Got a Friend." Jax was transfixed by the fingers on the steel strings, creating butterfly notes that burst off the wood and flew into our ears. The guitarist wasn't wearing a wedding ring, and I idly wondered if he might be a good boyfriend: he could teach Jax to play guitar, and I could help him pay to get his teeth capped.

I caught myself right away, and wanted to hit myself over the head with his guitar, like Quick Draw McGraw — El Kabong!

Jax and I read, walked the dogs, played with the kitty's tail, took naps, and then prepared dinner. Sam and Amy got back from *Avatar* in much less ecstatic moods than I had hoped. They were barely speaking, in fact. I had made Sam's favorite foods — steak, Caesar salad, roast potatoes — and lit candles, and managed to do this all with a squirmy baby in my arms, and I had been in a kind of vicarious romantic fantasy for Sam and Amy. Oh, well.

Sam announced, upon entering the house, "I may be running out of the Valentine's Day mood about now." My heart tumbled around. So I broke open the bubbly, Martinelli's sparkling cider, and tried to subtly manipulate them into being cheerful. But they were unhappy with each other, while I had gone to so much trouble and expense. I thought about taking Sam aside, as I could when he was a kid, and saying something spiritual like "Shape the fuck up." But he's a man, a father. We sort of got through it all — getting through stuff, I guess, is eighty percent of grace — and I didn't say anything about his bad character. I somehow held my tongue, while considering various appropriate forms of correction; I also focused on Jax, and breathed.

The three of them left at seven, thank God. I'm so in love with this baby, yet *dog*-tired every time he leaves. I don't know where that leaves the dogs. At any rate, the dogs, the kitty, and I had to take a pre-bedtime nap on the couch.

After Sam, Amy, and Jax left, I finally realized that I don't have the correction in me. Life is the correction. Life will correct Sam well, and unfortunately, it'll correct me, too. Life corrects harshly. Failure is the conduit.

I so felt for them: Sam and Amy were exhausted, as always, and Sam was pressured to the max with school, Amy, and Jax, on top of the grotesqueries of Valentine's Day. And even if they were both in free fall, I was not their parachute. God was. Gack. I hate that.

February 15

I called Sam after the Valentine's Day debacle and had a victory.

I did not say that I was very disappointed, and that he needed to change.

I did not say, You are awful, and men are pigs.

I said it had made me feel miserable for them to be so cold to each other in front of me and Jax — to harsh each other, as the teenagers say. Wait: Sam was still a teenager six months ago. I asked if next time he could try to rise to the occasion. He didn't say anything, but stayed on the phone.

I said I wasn't willing to be in a situation

where they were rude to each other. They got to have their relationship, and I got to say what I wouldn't tolerate, but it was bad for Jax, and I didn't want to set myself up again.

Sam said, "Well, then don't." He added that he was sorry, and he heard me.

After a moment, I said I appreciated that we could have this difficult conversation, and that I was grateful he was sticking it out with me, letting me tell my truth, and that we hadn't hung up self-righteously. To lighten the mood, I said that I actually must have done something right.

There was a pause, and he said, "No. Not really. Not that *I* can think of." Oh, Sam. We laughed, and that is baby progress, healing, a grace note.

February 16
Jax will be seven months old in four days. The speed of this makes a mockery of all life. So I bought a cake. Stevo, Clara, and Neshama came to tea to celebrate, early, along with Amy and Jax. Jax's baby wobble was gone, the gyroscopic tremor like Katharine Hepburn at the end. Now he was focused and unwavering. His eyes still seemed enormous, even though his head is bigger and his face has filled out. He's still

a little man, but not that wizened old man of infancy, who looked like medieval paintings of babies. Stevo said he looks like someone who might have a wallet, or back pockets. "Manolito," he pleaded, "lend me a sawbuck." Jax thought it over before declining. His gestures are slow and deliberate. *He's* the one deciding whom to look at, where his gaze is going to land. Before, people would try charming him, making funny faces and sounds to get his attention, but now he's not having any of it. Now *he's* choosing. You know, mostly.

Two major new developments: First, he has clapped a number of times, which is thrilling for him and for us, because it takes so much for hands to come together perfectly flat. There are so many moving parts, and many obstacles that could get in the way — your nose, for instance. Just weeks ago, before I left for India, it was still spaz and flail, herky-jerk.

And second, his raspberry is more mature, less spitty and spluttery, less Chris Matthews, more Artie Shaw. It's a dry, intentional, buzzing vibration, and he is transfixed by this ability, and looks primed to capitalize on it, as if he might just pick up a clarinet and play "Begin the Beguine," with a hat on the ground at his feet for tips.

February 17

On the day of my favorite St. Andrew church service, when Amy asked if I could babysit Jax, it was all I could do to turn her down. I had seen them the day before, and then two days before that at St. Andrew. When I was teaching Sunday school, Jax was crawling around while Amy got the crafts projects and the food together for the big kids, and all of a sudden he emerged from her purse, having opened up a little container of baby-junk-food sweet-potato bits, which he was shoving into his mouth; he had so much drool on his hands that they were sticking to him, and he looked like a wino.

I thought, Boy, is that my grandson or what?

Every time I manage to say no to Amy or Sam about babysitting Jax, someone should give me money, or the fish you use to train seals. It is hard to pass up any chance to be with him, but Ash Wednesday is more important to me than Christmas, or even Easter. It is such a poignant night of hymns, laments, Scripture, and testimony from the altar about ways in which we are desperate to change. We rend a strip of cloth, daub our foreheads with ashes. There are never more than fifteen people, and usually fewer.

I usually mention my tiny control issues at the altar. Also, my vanity and self-loathing.

Yet even though I have not missed this service in twenty years, I was really bushed by dinnertime, and almost didn't go. Then, at the last minute, I forcibly roused myself, all but holding a gun to my head, and drove to Marin City. When I arrived, there were eight women and my pastor, Veronica, who explained that the people in the Wednesday-night Bible study group had written their own psalms, and would share them tonight. Afterward, in an hour or so, we would have the ash service.

But, but, but — she'd *said,* during Sunday worship, that we would be having our annual Ash Wednesday celebration. *This* was some sort of Build-A-Bear Workshop. I did not want to hear homemade psalms. I wanted real psalms, from the Old Testament, and my damn ashes.

So I left.

I was so disappointed and confused that I started crying in the parking lot, and my mind was a pinball machine of exasperation with myself, and all of life. In addition, I decided briefly that I would leave St. Andrew entirely and take my very spiritually evolved self — and my money — to another church, where they did things properly.

But then I heard the voice of God. It said gently: Stop. Go back in. Surrender your will.

Instead, I headed to the Clinique counter at Macy's.

After I parked, I heard the voice again: Honey, go back.

I really *wanted* to want to do this: the Day of Ashes is about seeing how crazy and lonely we are, when left to our own devices. But I wasn't done with my best efforts yet.

I hesitated in the parking lot. And I almost went back. Instead, I bought a forty-five-dollar tinted skin lotion. I got a free sample of eye cream. Then I went home.

The sweet dogs tried to comfort me and I was pissy with them. It was not until I hurt Lily's feelings and told her to back off that I said to God, "I think I'm done. I want to come back." But I couldn't think of how to do that, so I called Tom.

He said, "We all enjoy stories of your hysteria and shallowness."

"Will you talk to me about Ash Wednesday?"

He said, "Everyone hates you."

"I get so goddamn sick of myself," I said.

"Ashes are about remembering that we came from dust, and to dust we will return," he said. "We're all going to die. Our loved ones will die. But we can repent, and change, become more kind, and present to life — because left to ourselves, we all get burnt out. Think of when you were drinking, feeling better and better as the night progressed — and then how you'd wake up with the taste of ash in your mouth."

"What does it mean liturgically?"

"It means, I would go door-to-door and explain to your neighbors that now is the time to take down the damn outdoor Christmas lights. Starting tonight, we let go of that which is past, and enter the new season, as a community, as we begin our observation of Easter. We're going to let go of everything that got us here, our own best thinking. Liturgically, it means that we say, 'Let's change our lives, again, try to be kinder people, again, try not to be such assholes.'

"And it means, as a community, we would *all* like to see some improvement from a certain writer in Marin."

I laughed, and ate a cherry Tootsie Pop, slowly, and this was how I shook off for a little while the taste of ashes that covers me.

February 19, Interview with Sam
"Sam, tell me what he is like now, at seven

months old."

"He's a totally roaring, rocking, kicking Godzilla child — like he's part of a World Series crowd that's gone wild. He's gotten such focus and will, and then Amy and I have these clashes of will, so it's like we're two alpha-male gorillas, trying to raise Godzilla.

"What's changed in the last few months is that the buck really stops here — with me. The problem has to stop at this chain of command. I'm not going to turn over my problems to you — to my *mother* — and say, 'I just can't take it anymore.' Now I automatically feel, 'Let's just get it done.' Before, I could perfectly imagine an elaborate drawing or plan, and then stall forever on creating it. Now I know I need to not put it off. With a horrible diaper, before, I might wait for Amy to discover it and deal with it, which was chickenshit. Now, like I said, the buck stops here. Just do it.

"Boy, we've come a long way from those first black-tar poops — now they're pretty human, kind of manly. Now, because he's so grown-up and can do so many things and engage with us, I think, 'Why am I wiping some other guy's ass? What's wrong with this picture?' Before, he was so helpless, but no more. I tell him, 'I am NOT going to be doing this for much longer.'

"Today he was on my lap being happy and playful with me for a long time, and then he wanted to crawl off and do his own thing. I let him go. Wow. Now he wants to *go* somewhere. Before, there was no somewhere else. Now, he might want to go to his bouncy saucer. And he totally wants to, with conviction, like when one of the dogs wants to go out — he doesn't give up or forget about it. It's like he's going, 'Hey, dude. What does it take for a guy to get put in his bouncy saucer around here?' "

"How has your relationship with God changed since you became a father?"

"Well, obviously now I know what it feels like to be a father. So I know how my heavenly father feels about me — so loving and protective, wanting me to make something great of my one precious life.

"I wouldn't even have to think about giving my life for Jax's. In a split second, I'd say: 'Oh, here — take it.'

"Our connection is so deep — it's partly because I saw him when he was just a speck inside Amy, and I saw her, every step of the way, growing bigger with him — and then all those ultrasound photos of him inside her. And now this: Godzilla. That's pretty profound to watch him grow from a speck.

He and I are made of the same flow, the same stock, the same material, so we're almost like the same thing. Plus we have the same heavenly father, so we're also like brothers on earth together.

"I think about God constantly, as much as I think about Jax. It's actually symbiotic — if I think about God, it means that Jax will have a sweet outcome, because I'll be a sweeter father.

"I got the two main prayers from you, 'Help help,' and 'Thank you thank you,' but I pray now with more detail than that. Now I know God has a tool crib, and I can borrow from it. I say, 'Hey, God, lend me some patience,' or I pray for Him to lend me some perseverance so I can see my inventions through to the marketplace. The only problem for me is remembering to ask for the loan. Oh, and maybe patience.

"Like, say I have to get rid of an imperfection in a Maple Cube for class — a tiny excess bit of wood that I need to sand or saw off if I want an A. It has to be perfectly square and plumb. So Sam's hands are going to be shaking, because I get anxious and I'll have bad self-esteem. Then I remember God has a tool crib. So I'll say, 'Hey, could you lend me your steady hands?' "

February 23

Sam and Amy called yesterday, and both were in tears of exhaustion, and Jax was sobbing in the background, and Amy said in a tiny voice, "You know how you keep offering us Sleeping Through the Night Boot Camp? Could that start tonight? Can we come over right now?"

I taught Sam to sleep through the night when he was a few months old, because babies' stomachs can hold enough milk to see them through and I was at the end of my rope. You nurse them at bedtime, put them down, and when they sob inconsolably, you go in and tell them what a good job they are doing. But you do not pick them up. It is one of the hardest things I have ever done, and the best. It makes you fall in love with your baby again.

Last night Jax did great. Amy was piteous but committed, and I was coldhearted and clinical about the whole thing — "Do *not* touch the baby, Amy. Step away from the baby. He has plenty of milk in his tummy to last the night. And do not sing to him, either, or he will expect it every night."

Amy did great, too, and I did not crack under the strain, until Jax woke up at ten and sobbed. Amy went in, gave him assurances, and then went into my office to use my computer. Jax kept crying, and finally I sneaked like a thief into the guest room, where he was sleeping, lifted him out of his crib for a few minutes, calmed him down. I put him back, and was tiptoeing out of the room when Amy appeared at the door. "Annie," she said angrily, and gave me a very bad look. He cried for twenty minutes, and then he stopped. He began to sob again in the middle of the night, and it woke me, and I tiptoed into the kitchen to listen, and I heard Amy saying in the guest room, "You are doing a great job, Jax. I'm right here, but I'm not going to pick you up." I went back to bed, and after a few minutes, he stopped crying.

I did okay when she put him down for his morning nap — boy, she is tough, and she is in with him now, nursing him before the gulag door slams shut for ten or fifteen minutes.

He sobbed during his afternoon nap, when Amy was doing Facebook on my computer. I crept in and patted him. It was not enough, and I sneaked out.

Then I went to find Amy at my computer, hung my head, and said, "I patted him." She was mad. You'd have thought I'd given him IV Valium. "Jeez," I said. "I just patted him!"

I'm in disgrace now, and cannot be trusted.

She told me that I have to admit in this journal that I sneak around like a dog, breaking the only boot-camp rule.

My friend Lizzy, who has grandchildren, happened to e-mail me today, and I replied and told her what was going on, what a generally awful, weak person I am, but also how contrite. She wrote back: "You are right about having to let Jax cry it out, but it is hard. As a grandma, I have done what you did. I struggled, and backslid. Remember, I called myself the Neville Chamberlain of the nursery — peace at any price. Don't be mean to yourself, though. You told old athe-ist me once that this is the only sin."

February 25
Last night Jax got himself to sleep after ten minutes of crying, and then slept through the night. He passed out after crying a few minutes for both naps today. We all like him again and have decided to renew his lease.

February 28
Today was Millard's memorial service, at a bigger house across the street from my cousin Ricky's, where Millard had lived. The timing couldn't have been worse: two days

ago, I went to my dermatologist for my annual melanoma check, and she offered to burn some age spots and precancerous things off my face, and then she really got into it, and I wasn't thinking about how awful and scabby I would look for the next few days. So today I woke looking like Dick Cheney's best friend, that poor Mr. Whittington, after Cheney blasted him in the face with quail shot while hunting. Also, Amy and Jax are going to visit the relatives in Chicago for two weeks. Sam is distressed, as it is too long for him and Jax to be apart, but Amy has adamantly insisted on this arrangement, and that is that. She has a will like no other. Luckily, she also has a cosmetology license, and so, upon seeing my crazy duck-hunter face, she started slapping unguents and foundations and powders on me, until I was presentable, in a *Six Feet Under* kind of way.

We all hiked together from my house — Neshama, Stevo, Annette, Clara, Sam, Amy, Jax; we are such a funny family. I got happy again. Sam told us as we walked that after Sleeping Through the Night Boot Camp, Jax has come into his own. Before that, if you said his name, he'd look right over. Now, if he's involved with something, like his plastic phone or keys, and you call out to him, he'll look up eventually, like he's working on a presentation and time is money. Like he'll have his people call your people.

Dozens of people had gathered, relatives of all ages, old friends, aged and middle-aged professors from Millard's decades of teaching at the College of Marin. Some were unable to get up from their seats without young male volunteers and major construction-crane efforts. I have known many of them all my life, when their children were still at home and their spouses were alive. Now they were old, bruised by life, tweaked and achy but still whole, not to mention brilliant conversationally — in essence, like Millard was, and is.

Millard's Jewish relatives came, and people from my father's side, like my aunt Eleanor, whom Millard claimed as his sister-in-law once removed, and the former babies in the family, who were getting along now, all of whom I've been eating holiday meals with my whole life. Jax, Clara, and my cousin Ricky's three kids were the new generation, and boy, did they look new, compared with us.

There were great buffet tables of fine food — good food had been so important to Millard's life. Fifty or so people bustled about;

three old professors sat on one couch the entire time. We were disparate elements of Millard's life, meeting in some cases for the first time, although I knew most people there. At some point, my cousin Kathy asked me to get everyone to sit down so our service could begin. You needed a cattle dog to round up all these people who wanted more food or another glass of wine, and I guess I was that cattle dog.

Millard's spirit came through the dry, funny stories about him — as a father, an uncle, a wild and inspiring teacher, and a friend — but people focused mostly on his love for Pat. My cousins talked about how he was with her, which was something that you don't see all that often on this side of things. He was so faithful in his love, even when she faded and was mentally diminished at the end. He honored and saluted her essence to the absolute end of her life, and of his. In my eulogy I said that I loved his personality combinations, his being brilliant and yet patient, learned and ethereal, loving and caustic, and his being down-to-earth, whether he was trying once again to help you understand Einstein's theory of relativity, or a unified field theory, or the quirks and madness and genius of the Tudor dynasty — or trying to help you save a chicken stew over the phone, or nagging you into having another helping of his latest and greatest new curry, and then accusing you of anti-Semitism if you declined. I loved his total devotion to and belief in family, in gathering, meeting, mourning, celebrating, and eating — and eating and eating. He loved the very old people in our family, and the babies, and the babies of the babies. He always remembered the ancestors. My brother John said that watching his love and devotion to my funny, bossy aunt Pat over the years was probably the most spiritual aspect of my family while he was growing up. I remember Millard and Pat coming to visit my mom a few days before she died, and how impatient Pat was, as usual, with my mom — how exasperating she found her, even when she was just lying quietly in a nursing home — and I remember how patient Millard was with both of them. He had always seen, through the decades, how hard my mom's life was, and he was kindly and inclusive. My mother always felt what I always felt — that Millard thought she was wonderful, just as she was, and who she was, which was, in a word, family.

Sam, Amy, Jax, Clara, Stevo, and Neshama huddled together, joined by John, whom we adore but who lives a distance away and rarely makes appearances at family gatherings. Jax, in Amy's lap in an easy chair near the fire, was dressed in teddy-bear football sweats, instead of the more formal baby wear I would have selected. It was to him, and not Millard, that we kept returning. Millard was the old year; Jax was the new.

Jax was comfortable, social, solid, observant, like Millard, and never cried. We took turns playing with him, and Sam walked around with him proudly, rocking him in his arms while answering people's questions. "He's seven months. . . . Oh, *me?* I'm twenty."

Outside the huge windows were eucalyptus, bay laurel, the northern face and hills of Tamalpais. The service was a mix of sweet, uncomfortable, hilarious, touching. There was a sense of grace and economy, as had distinguished Millard's departure.

Jax peeped and made farting noises, and everyone who held him returned him at the first sign of fuss to the space station of his mom in the easy chair.

People were sort of organically ready to go when everyone had finished speaking. I was reminded of the Four Immutable Laws of the Spirit: Whoever is present are the right people. Whenever it begins is the right time. Whatever happens is the only thing that could have happened. And when it's over, it's over. It was over.

My wing of the family stayed clustered around the easy chair where Jax orbited in Amy's lap, first nursing, then sitting up to see us all from the orbit of Amy: planet and moon.

March 6

I loved Millard's memorial so much, but have been in mental disarray ever since, especially in the four days since Amy and Jax left. They will be gone ten more days. We haven't heard from her yet. I know she is busy today, as it is her friend Amanda's twenty-first birthday, and knowing this makes it easier for me to focus on keeping the patient comfortable: I made myself soup, put clean sheets on the bed, and took a nap. Then I called Doug, who lives only a few miles from where Amy and Jax were staying, and asked if he could drive by and take some photos of Jax with his cell phone and send them to me.

"Poor Nana," Doug said.

"We haven't heard a word from her since she left. Sam hasn't gotten to talk to Jax in four days!"

"And this would be your business because . . . ?"

I was silent.

"Lower the bar of expectations," he enthused. "Secret of life."

I called Stevo to see if he and Clara could come by for a house call. He asked what he could bring.

"Just Clara," I said. "Oh, and some sweet-and-sour pork. Perhaps a small side of chow mein."

"Anything else?"

"The merest hint of Ben and Jerry's New York Super Fudge Chunk."

As soon as Stevo walked in with a bag of Chinese takeout and the ice cream, and Clara plopped her gangly seven-year-old self into my lap at the table, I knew I was going to be okay.

Clara is smart, and lovely in the way only young girls can be, bright colors inside and out. She's a big kid now, a tall, stylish girl, but her skin is just as vibrational as when she was Jax's age. It does not bear one scar or sag of life, and it fits perfectly. It hasn't started to lump up like an old whale's, as happens to the skin of certain people I could mention, i.e., me. Clara wore pedal pushers. I was dressed for Mongolia, and Stevo, not quite fifty, was in between.

229

They stayed and drew with me for a couple of hours. I finished off the sweet-and-sour for my afternoon snack, had some New York Super Fudge Chunk for dinner, and later, in bed, ate the last of the chow mein, from the box, with chopsticks, the way happy people in the movies always do.

March 7
It is the most important date in the Christian calendar: the Academy Awards. Neshama and I are going to watch them with Bill and Emmy Smith in San Rafael, as I have for twenty-plus years. There will be grilled chicken breast sandwiches tonight, with avocado and balsamic onion and Em's famous homemade aïoli, and chocolates, and one-bite perfect fruit tarts in tiny paper undies that I picked up at the bakery after church.

Church was lifesaving, as usual, from the minute the choir filed in with a sense of calm and centeredness. They come to open their souls and their hearts, and they opened their mouths to sing the processional. I am always hungry for the choir's music, and to be held by community and spirit, and I loved every minute — it was like going to the gas station to be filled up for the week. But let's be honest: I was just killing time.

Nothing can compare to the spiritual majesty of the Oscars.

March 14

It has all been downhill since last Sunday. I called Amy a few more times while she was in Chicago, to check in, but she didn't pick up or call me back. I practiced releasing her. It went poorly. I don't know why she won't call or text. Sam and I have been working and distracting ourselves, Sam at school, and me doing interviews for a book tour I start in a few weeks.

As the days pass, we are both in better moods, because Amy and Jax will be home in two days.

I called Neshama to talk about how frustrated I am with Amy, for leaving for so long and for not returning my calls, and she did not try to fix me, or get me to see the light, which is that Amy's grandmother, whom she loves deeply, won't be around much longer, and that Amy's parents get to see the baby only every few months. And because she did not shove this down my throat, this dawned on me. Neshama volunteered to come over if I needed company. I asked whether she would go to the Fijian church with me, in the next town over; I've wanted to visit ever since I heard the harmonies waft out one afternoon while I was walking by. Neshama was at my house an hour later, game for anything, and we drove to the strange church in the next town.

These were big people! Maybe there has to be a big container for all that enormous sound. And also maybe it is their island make-up, all those starchy roots and poi. On such exposed land, perhaps it helps to be tethered, so the wind doesn't blow you away to neighboring islands. The extra weight provides lots of buoyancy for swimming, and there's more of you left in case nature shuts down and all the fish die. At any rate, many of the people here were really large, brown and gorgeous.

Some of the men were wearing skirts. (I was a little curious about the underwear, because the Scots in their kilts are rumored not to wear any. But as I was here to worship God, I tried not to think about this.)

There were forty people or so, and we were welcomed like the prodigals we were. The Scripture readings were in Fijian and then English; the people sang in Fijian, and their harmonies reminded me of Soweto. This kind of beauty softens you and expands you, which is good, but of course it makes you vulnerable to all sorts of horrible things, like, oh, feelings. And being in your body.

The harmonies are soul tenderizers. They get right in there, into the fibers of your being, into the usually armored muscles and chambers, and open you up with awe, just as happens at St. Andrew or the Taj Mahal.

When they sang "Holy, Holy, Holy," it sounded like "Gormu Gormu Gormu," but what got into me was that we are together in the universal love of God, on the same page, in creation, in hardship, in silence and out loud.

What got into me here, and what gets into me at St. Andrew, was the combination of supplication and deep, intimate conversation with something that listens.

The woman behind us had a huge stretched mouth trimmed in bright red lipstick. She looked about my age; she was beautiful, loudly crying out a stirring, impassioned prayer of pain and trust wedded together.

The Fijian language is clickety and crickety. The service was much like St. Andrew, otherworldly and yet down-to-earth. The harmonies were round, and had solidity, without interpretation, so spirit came out big and solid. There was no piano, so people tuned in to one another's voices, and their sound was strong and assured, but also had a great brightness and glitter. The channel was from deep down inside the earth; it came up through the crust, to the ground, and up through our feet and up through our chests and hearts and up our throats and out of our mouths, and it surrounded everyone like a blanket, and it somehow also rose through the air, to the sky, to the stars, this sound that had come up through our rough feet.

March 16
I was still high from the Fijian church on Tuesday, when Sam called to say that Amy was not coming home as scheduled, for a number of mysterious reasons. He was angry that she would not level with him, but philosophical: he had massive midterm assignments, and thought maybe it would turn out for the best.

"You don't know why she is staying? And when is she coming back, then?" I asked sweetly, while idly wondering how much of my retirement savings we could spend pursuing a legal assault on her.

He didn't know the answer to either question. She'd said she would be back soon.

I didn't want to call Bonnie, because she would say that something beautiful was being revealed, and that things were unfolding in a perfect way, and wasn't it touching that

234

everywhere Jax went, he was blessed by the love of family, in this case Amy's Chicago relatives?

I so do not want to hear this. Or that Sam and Amy had to work this out, and that Sam is not me. That there is their life, and there is mine, where I am learning to be a grandmother. That Jax has other grandparents, who love him like I do, and who've had to bear living far away, and have done so with equanimity.

I was certainly in no mood to hear that sort of shit, at all.

So instead of calling Bonnie, I went for a walk with the dogs, and I ran into a lawyer I know. He asked how I was. I told him that Amy kept postponing her return, and how afraid I was that she might take off with Jax someday, and not come back.

We had a nice invigorating discussion about how Sam and Amy needed a mediator to help them work out custody issues, and the lawyer said I was right to be bothered by Amy's seemingly arbitrary decision to stay longer. I felt better when we said good-bye. It was great to be right. Really, it's the most important thing — to be right, and to know whom to blame.

March 18

Amy called Sam an hour ago to say she is not coming home today, either.

I was finally forced to call horrible Bonnie. I told her that if she said that this was between Sam and Amy, I was hanging up. Bonnie thought this was very funny and charming. She and Tom both enjoy the heck out of me.

She did say that this was their life — their grand adventure. That this was about their family, and their home, their choices; for instance, if I went over and saw dirty dishes in the sink, I must leave them. She added, "Honey, I promise, if Amy and Jax stay in Chicago, or move there after coming back here briefly, your love for Jax and his for you do not require proximity. Jax's and your love for each other is indelible, and eternal."

Oh, stop. My happiness depends on my having Jax nearby, and on Sam's getting to see him every day, and on both of us getting to hear him laugh all the time, and watch him sleep, and smell that heavenly hair. Duh.

"Oh, dearest," she said. I know that when she calls me "dearest" I am doomed. "You have been on a bit of a run, huh? Trying to be everyone's rock and savior, needing to be invaluable, so Amy won't leave with Jax.

But Amy leaves anyway, and takes Jax with her, because she misses her family and friends and they miss her, and they need to be together as much as possible."

"But what should I do?" I wailed. "She doesn't return our calls or texts. We're her family, too."

"You're not going to like this. But you need to deal with the fact that she is young, and has free will, and roots that are thousands of miles away. Don't be a big baby. She is not your problem. Go look in the mirror, my honey. You are in withdrawal. You're in victim mode. And that has nothing to do with Amy. That's lifelong. You need radical self-care and acceptance."

"I feel exposed and needy and repulsive."

"Fabulous! Now we're starting to get somewhere. We can address this, and why your good ideas cannot help. *Or* you can stay in blame-and-rescue."

This was a rather stunning and rude view of my suffering.

I thought it over. "Listen," I said. "Can I get back to you on this?"

March 19
Trudy called Sam from North Carolina to say that Amy was sick with a fever, which the doctors had at first not been able to

diagnose; she was better now, on a high dose of antibiotics and pain meds. Of course, Trudy was prepared to fly to Chicago if Amy got worse, but it seemed that she was on the mend.

When Sam told me this, my first thought was that I should get on a plane and fly to her side and be Florence Nightingale. Then I remembered that I had facetiously considered contacting a lawyer. Then I thought about how great a high level of pain meds would be about now. Finally I called it a day, and got in bed with a book, and stroked my own shoulder and said, "There, there."

March 20
When I woke up, there was a group e-mail waiting for me from a friend. I almost deleted it, as I do all group mailings. But instead, when I opened it, I saw a picture of Jesus looking right at me, and the caption "I can't help you with your problem as long as you've got it in a half nelson."

March 21
Sam phoned to say that Amy was better, her fever was gone, and she would be home in the next couple of days.

"Oh, well, that's nice," I said, sweet as pie. "What *ev.*"

Sam laughed. "I love you," he said. "You're so great. You're very comical and entertaining."

I have to start dealing with Sam and Amy as a pair, and stop cushioning them. As a child I was always the ball bearings for my whole family; I thought I was indispensable to their survival, preventing hard metal from grinding against hard metal, so the family didn't come to a broken, screeching, metallic halt. This is a role I am very comfortable in, and in which I excel.

It was one of my jobs as a child — along with marriage counseling, and raising my younger brother. Come to think of it, it didn't work all that well then. I don't suppose it will now, either. The job of a good parent is to be dispensable. No one remembered to tell my parents that, but I know it is true.

It's not morally right to make yourself indispensable.

I called Tom and asked his advice. "My advice would be for you to leave them the fuck alone." I wrote this down on an index card.

March 22
My beloved Doug flew in from Chicago, out of the blue, and stayed overnight with

me: something had come up that he had to take care of. Sam said that to him, this constitutes a brown-bag miracle. Doug knows better than anyone the details of our family drama. He knows me the way only a few people can know you your whole life.

We hung out on the couch with the dogs, overate, and talked into the night.

"Oh, baby," he said. "Tom was right. You have to leave them alone."

"But I could help them sort out some stuff. I have great ideas."

"You do have excellent ideas, honey. And that is why you should keep those precious thoughts to yourself. What's right for us is to lop off some of the tentacles we have wrapped around our kids. I've had to do that, too. Otherwise, we oppress them."

I dug the fingers of one hand into my face, and attempted to pull off my nose and lips, but Doug loosened my grip. "This is hard," he said. "How could you have been ready to be a grandmother any more than Sam was ready to be a father?" I shrugged. "But honey? Here we are."

I got in bed late with the dogs and cat, and lay in the dark praying and thinking. It is a violation of trust to use your kids as caulking for the cracks in you. So I said to God, Fine, have it your way. What ev.

It's a new prayer, to add to the other two, Help me, and Thank You: What ev. I should get this tattooed on my shoulder, "Help me, thank you, what ev, and lower the bar."

March 23
God is my witness: Sam woke me at six to say that Amy and Jax are flying home today. Doug was already up, because he was on Chicago time, and I bounced into his room like Pogo Stick Girl to tell him my good news. He was happy for my temporary reprieve, but he knew it was just that, a stay of execution, and I knew that, too. We made tortillas with cheese and avocado for breakfast, and read *The New York Times* in cheerful silence.

March 24
Sam called from school to say that Amy and Jax got in last night, and Jax was great, hilarious, so cute you couldn't stand it.

I wanted to go into San Francisco and be Big Mama to Amy, plus God, the Bank, and a Molly Maid, from the local cleaning-lady company, but instead I called her. She was distant. I asked if I could come in and take them shopping for food. She agreed. So I did.

Seeing Jax, in his brown beauty and charm

and loveliness, gave me a big hit of peace. I think the shadow side of being a grandparent is that the child becomes like an ATM of self-respect and completion. You can be at your worst mentally, with grudges, anxiety, and no self-esteem, then spend five minutes with the Unit and feel instantly restored. It is a form of love addiction. There are twelve-step programs to stop using other people to fill up your holes.

Oh, well. Too bad, so sad. Hand over that kid! I will deal with this soon.

Jax threw himself at me after a few moments of shyness, such a big boy, very toothy, with longer, thicker dark hair, crawling around like an all-terrain vehicle. He looks tall when standing, but when he crawls, he looks like the Prince of the Pillbugs, all round rolled-up aerodynamic thrust.

We hung out in their apartment for half an hour, and though Sam had gotten it all picked up, it needed a deep cleaning, and I did not say a word or offer to help. I said to myself, sternly: It is their house. Their house — what a concept.

I do not really believe it for a second.

I have tried to accept for twenty years that Sam is not an extension of me, that children have their own autonomous existence, and

242

242

that parents have the moral obligation to help them discover this. But this should not apply to me and Jax, too, since I am once removed; it applies only to Sam and me. All the grandparents I know have glommed on to the grandchildren, like barnacles with credit cards, and yellow rubber gloves for doing their dishes. And it is good.

Amy, Jax, and I went to Safeway for groceries. While Amy filled the cart to overflowing, I got to hold Jax and explain how essential each of the products was, and suck up the smells of his hair and neck like an anteater.

The good news was that in the hours we spent together, the only time money changed hands was when I picked up the grocery bill. The bad news is that it was close to three hundred dollars.

I played with Jax while Amy put the groceries away. I intentionally, heroically, did not instigate a single interesting conversation. Our time together was awkward. But we did okay, and that is a lot. There is going to be hard work ahead of us, even though I love her deeply and would do almost anything for her; and I know that she loves me deeply and would do almost anything for me. It's like the story of Ruth and her mother-in-law, Naomi, without the unim-

peachable characters. We are both so im-
peachable, willful, damaged. But as they say,
more will be revealed. Whoever "they" is.

March 25, Interview with Sam
"Sam? Having just spent forty-eight hours
with Jax, after having not seen him for a
while, how has he changed?"

"Well, you are right that he is an ATV
now, or an SUV. He's gone from needing
perfect conditions in order to scooch across
the floor, to having four-wheel drive. There
is nothing on the ground, no obstacle at all,
that he can't get over. You'll see — at your
house, he will be able to crawl over the dogs.

"Before, if there was something on the
floor that he wanted when he had pulled
himself up at the table, the only way he
could get it was to fall down. Now he can
lower himself from a standing position to
pick it up. Like, you might think you were
having a nice conversation with him while
he's standing, and then he remembers what
it is he wants, and he lowers himself to get
it, and then sees you on the way back, and
he's like, 'Oh, hi — there you are. I forgot
something. What were you saying?'

"He's very polite. I talk to him like he's
an adult, and he hears everything, and
listens patiently, but then something might

catch his eye. He doesn't interrupt anymore by flailing and grabbing for the object, but he'll see something out of the corner of his eye, and you can tell he is thinking, 'Oh, nice Daddy doesn't matter,' and he crawls away towards the object. I guess that's what it will be like more and more from now on.

"He's like part dog, part bat now, the way he uses his senses. The first test of anything is to taste it, and to measure it orally. Then the second test is to see how it sounds when he smashes it against other things.

"He's mellow and happy most of the time. He's peaceful, but like Bodhi in that he can accidentally hurt you with his love and that huge head.

"When you watch him watching things, it's like seeing the history of mankind and suddenly understanding where inspiration comes from, how humans are inspired to create just from watchfulness, without hard-and-fast preconceived positions on everything. Watching Jax watch stuff, you can see how Egyptian statues were created, or how Michelangelo saw David in the block of marble, or how all those inventions came to Leonardo da Vinci.

"These last weeks have been very hard, terribly painful, but part of being a man is to take the pain and make something out of it, like being able to grow, or having insights or ideas for art, or maybe just coming to be less of an asshole. Instead of dishing it out, or having to hurt others because of it. Because that's the worst thing."

March 26

I have been practicing being dispensable, and lowering the bar, which is good, as I have not heard from Amy since my drive-by.

I opened the Bible randomly and ended up on one of what Tom calls the Cursing Psalms, 109, a nice, juicy rage psalm — "You make me sick, may the dogs eat your bones." Or something like that — I have never been able to memorize Scripture. Tom told me a few weeks ago that Protestants need the Cursing Psalms much more than Catholics do, that we have a lot more to be angry about. When I asked him why, he said, "You don't have the daily joy of the papacy."

Remembering this is the only thing that has cheered me up so far today.

March 27

I was going a little stir-crazy earlier, wondering why I had not heard from Sam and Amy, but I tried not to butt in with my thinky thoughts, bribes, and offers. I know Amy is not glad to be back from Chicago, but she is not sure of much else right now — whether she will stick around San Francisco so she and Sam can raise Jax together.

Then she called to say she and Jax would be here at five with many loads of laundry, and they might stay over; I could have danced all night. Maybe I should take issue with these spur-of-the-moment visits, and instead set some boundaries.

Yeah, right. That's going to happen.

They both arrived with colds, but cheerful, and I was so in love with them that I didn't mind that they were shedding virus all over me. Jax sounded croupy, like a goose, but his appetite was good, and Amy said he seemed like himself again, and he scooched all over the living room, the furniture, and both of us. I took this at face value and remembered that it was *their* baby, *their* life story. That my job is to try not to keep trapping them in the web of my great wisdom, comforts, and fear. So I practiced letting go, although Jax's breathing did sound labored to me, and I may have possibly in the tiniest way mentioned this to Amy again; left to my own devices, I would have brought in the Medevac helicopter. But the story is also about my taking joys as they come, which is Jax on the move, my little SUV plowing across the floor, right over the dogs, like his daddy said he would.

March 28, Interview with Sam
Sam called nice and early to say that they wouldn't be coming to church, that Amy was still sick and trying to catch up on sleep on the couch, and he and Jax were lying in bed talking. I could hear Jax barking in the background, and I asked if he was better, and Sam said he was. So I spoke to myself in my silent guru voice: Release! Tuck in those tentacles! Breathe.

Sam said, "Do you want to do a little interview?"

"Yeah!"

"Because I can finally see that the way he grabs his bottle and sucks it in five different ways is a sign of his intelligence. He's like a little space alien, and his mouth is his major deductive tool. He flips bottles around — right now he's flipping around my water bottle — trying to figure out how to get the water out. And it fills me with respect for his process. I mean, he's been sticking things in his mouth since the very second he could, as his main survival instinct; but who knew it was developing into scientific inquiry? He used to slobber in a way that could be annoying, because you had to keep changing his shirts or bibs, but now he's doing it in a way that is teaching him all about life, and how things work. For me to interfere and try to get him to stop sucking on everything, shoving everything into his mouth, would be like telling an astronomer to stop staring through his telescope."

All was well with the world again, but when I got home from church, there was a message from Amy that Jax seemed to be having trouble breathing.

I texted back that they needed to take him to the emergency room. Amy texted that she'd take him to their doctor tomorrow when his office opened. I replied that it might be best to take him to the ER today.

Then I called, and said it offhandedly: Take him to the goddamn ER.

They did. When I didn't hear from them for a few hours, I naturally assumed Jax was in the ICU, after thoracic surgery, or hooked up to a heart-lung machine. Amy finally called to say there was no cell-phone reception in the ER. Jax did have croup, and was being given all the stuff I used to give Sam when he got asthma during a head cold — major meds like albuterol and steroids. Jax was doing fine, but the doctors wanted to watch him for a while. Amy made it clear that she would call when she could; there was no point in my calling, because there was no reception.

I was flooded with relief. But after I got off the phone, I wanted to jump up and down and shout, "Croup croup croup! I was right!" Because I'm human, which is to say crazy in some respects, and some people who shall remain nameless tricked me into loving them too deeply and ruined my life.

Then I had to wait for hours till I heard from them again. I kept gently reminding myself that they would call when they could, that there was no reception; that Jax was fine; that Jesus was right there in the ER with them, overseeing things with His gentle love. Then I remembered that He was with me, too, and loved me with my tentacles and schadenfreude just as much as He loved perfect Jax, which to me is the central mystery of my faith. So I stretched out on the couch with the dogs, the cat, and all the sections of the *Times* I hadn't read yet, and that is what grace looked like for a few hours.

At nine I began cracking under the strain of not hearing, so I called a friend whose kid has a brain tumor. She said I should try to stay out of the obsession and fear, because that morass is not helpful to live in.

It's like that joke about wrestling with pigs — you get hurt and dirty, while the pigs love it.

But what is the alternative? I asked.

"Well, you know," she said. "God and prayer. Faith."

"Oh!" I said, smiting my forehead. "Right."

I managed not to call Amy or Sam. I practiced releasing them to grow and find their own way. I did not become a voice that either of them would need to argue with or resist. Instead, they should listen to their son's breathing improve, and to the voices of doctors and nurses. What a concept. And I was doing pretty well, until nine-thirty, when I cracked, and called the ER. A nurse told me that Jax had just been discharged, and they were all headed home. "Oh, that's great," I said. "Pretty much what I expected."

Pretty much, except for the trach, and the iron lung.

Sam called not long after, to tell me that this great old doctor had said Jax was fine — he prescribed lots of medicine in case Jax got worse or had the same symptoms in the future. The doctor told them to keep an eye on Jax, and to see the pediatrician in the morning. "Mom, we both appreciate how calm you stayed through this," Sam said. "And how you didn't bother us at the hospital. It was kind of amazing."

"Oh" — I laughed — "not a big deal."

March 31
I am doing endless interviews with newspapers and radios in the cities to which I will be traveling on a book tour. This is how you prepare. Packing for a week away is nothing, as I bring only carry-on luggage. I always buy new underwear, in case I am involved in a plane crash. Best to be wearing nice fresh underpants in case you are *not* burned beyond recognition. I just bought a whole new batch, big and roomy like underpants a dancing bear might wear. Amy and Sam despair at my underwear whenever they take my clean clothes out of the dryer to put their own in. They do not think I can ever get a good boyfriend with underpants like these. When Sam was six or seven, one of his babysitters, a beautiful teenager, was helping me fold my laundry, and she picked up a pair of my underwear. Looking very worried, she said, "Do they even *make* them bigger than these?" I told her, "Oh, honey, you just wait."

April 2

My friend Mary is staying here with me for five days. We met thirty-five years ago in Bolinas, were instantly inseparable, and spent years drinking and taking acid together, and now she can have a glass of wine every so often, without needing to finish the bottle. I don't have this in me. I stopped almost twenty-four years ago. We lost touch for years, but now we are just as close as we ever were. She is Catholic, a big blonde with four grandchildren and a nephew who is getting a bone marrow transplant next week, for his leukemia. Today I took her and Jax into San Francisco for the Good Friday service at Mission Dolores, one of the early Spanish missions founded by Junípero Serra.

The service was in both Spanish and English, spoken by a handsome Hispanic priest. There were very few white people in the crowd of several hundred. Jax was sound asleep in my arms most of the time, and he seemed unusually small in that huge, glorious stained-glass space. His lips were pooched out, his cheeks were rosy and red, and he snorfled in his sleep. When he finally woke up and got his bearings, such as they were, he made that beautiful gesture of tucking his head under his wings with shyness. I feel like doing that all the time, ducking down and hiding my face, except that mature, together, confident adults don't do that.

He was awake for the last three Stations of the Cross. I love the ritual. It is like a nature hike: Here is a redwood, it loses its needles. . . . Here is a redwing blackbird. Also, it is all of life — you walk, you fall, you get up, you go on, you fall, you get up, you go on, you die, you resurrect. Mary was teary about her nephew, and I whispered to her the great line that we are Easter people living in a Good Friday world. The depth and the song of the Spanish language reminded me of the Fijian church: the supplication, and pain, and people having someplace to be together.

Jax flirted with an old Hispanic man in the aisle next to me, who put his leathery fingers near his ears and waggled them, then flew a plane or a bee all over his own airspace, up and down, up and down. This made Jax laugh, drop his eyes like a coquette, and dip his face back down under my wing.

April 7
I believe I am in Boston. The first question every interviewer in every medium has

254

asked is: "How do you like being a grand-mother?" I wrote a piece in February for the *Los Angeles Times* in which I mentioned that my son had had a son. I respond that it is a blessing, and do not go into anything interesting, like the complexity of it all, and the struggles; I say only that Jax is the third great love of my life, along with Sam and Jesus.

News of Jax is a showstopper. People think Sam must be sixteen by now.

The second or third question is about why I used the word "bird" in a title for the second time; this is just not right. What is it about me and birds?

It is a good question, although asked with some suspicion, as if I were capitalizing on the earlier book. There are birds throughout every book I've written. My father was an avid bird-watcher. He did not believe in God or read the Bible, but he believed in birds and read all of Audubon. I grew up believing that birds were of supreme value and beauty. That if you studied and ob-served them, you could learn a great deal about life.

I said in another book that if birdsong were the only proof of a bigger, invisible re-ality, that would be enough for me.

What's so great about birds, besides their

beauty, is that they are very different from us — we are so earthbound and they are so free — and yet so similar, especially to our children in their vulnerability. The small ones you might crush, and the big ones soar like little gods, pelicans skimming the surf, eagles and hawks as high in the sky as stars. Big ones might peck your eyes out or dive-bomb you. They're such alien creatures, so pretty, yet they spring from dinosaurs. And you can never look a bird in the eyes — their eyes are on either side of their heads, and they are so quizzical. They have to be — they are prey, and yet so hungry, like teen-agers; like us.

April 8

Last night, in a huge church outside Decatur, Georgia, where I was having a reading, some people asked me if I could go out with them for coffee and birthday cake. Temporarily unable to remember what city I was in, I said, "I just want to go back to — wherever it is that I am." Then I realized that this was possibly the most brilliant thing I have ever said. All I have to do for a shot at salvation is go back to where I am, and that means wherever my feet are, not my poor old pinball head.

Today is my father's eighty-sixth birthday.

He has been dead thirty years.

April 10
Today is my fifty-sixth birthday. I am in my
hotel room after my reading tonight, flying
home at dawn. My publisher sent me balloons and an entire chocolate cake. The
cake was like having a big rattlesnake on the
dresser. Finally I called room service and
ordered three scoops of sorbet. When the
woman from room service arrived, I asked
if I could give her this fancy chocolate cake
that said "Annie" on it, for her family. She
was glad to take it away, after I removed the
candles and made sure to pocket the match-
book. The single most radical thing I know,
which took me only forty-plus years to
learn, is that I get to take care of myself. Of
course, Amy and Sam get to take care of
themselves, too; so this is not great. But I
am not a victim of this: I do get to take care
of me, and so I put three candles onto my
balls of sorbet, and lit them, like prayer
candles in a cathedral: lemon, mango, raspberry.

April 11
I did housework today on my only day home
from the book tour, and it was lovely,
monk's work: I swept, folded laundry,

repacked for Seattle, walked the dogs, paid bills, and this has all made me calm and happy. It took nearly ten minutes to clean up Jax's drool-crust from the glass table in the living room. The drool-crust is like evidence that space aliens would leave behind on furniture after they abducted the earthlings in the house. And when I got it perfectly drool-crust clean, Amy, Jax, and Sam burst through the front door, followed not long after by Stevo, Annette, and Clara, with a carrot cake and balloons.

April 20
Jax is nine months old today, and I am sick from the book tour, mentally stuffed and with a bad cough, sore throat, no energy. But Amy needed to drop Jax off in the late afternoon so she could do errands and take some time for herself.

I took Jax to the park across the street on my shoulders, like a little big boy. My first memories are of my dad holding on to my ankles as we walked up to old St. Hillary's to look for sticky monkey flowers, which grow in these parts. Jax and I went on an owl prowl, staring up from beneath the branches of a redwood and a sycamore, with me calling up, "Whoooo, whoooo," to summon them. We have never once seen an owl, but always see other kinds of birds. I am teaching him to hug trees, which Sam does not quite approve of, being more conservative than I am in this regard.

When we were back home, I gave him a bottle of warm formula, and he fell asleep burrowed against my chest. I felt quiet, peaceful joy: my pastor Veronica says that peace is joy at rest, and joy is peace on its feet. Amy is a good mother, Sam is blowing me away with his arduous studies and sturdy fathering, Jax is the mellowest baby I've ever known. Riding on someone's shoulders, stopping to touch redwood bark — those were such crystallizing moments in my childhood and in Sam's, and now they are in Jax's, and will come and come. His sweetness and growing powers of observation make everything worth it, even the three weeks when Amy took him to Chicago, and the difficulty of constantly having to release Sam and Amy to their own destiny, to the immediacy of their groping, lurching, unfinished lives. But we somehow keep coming through. I listened to Jax snore. He's so snuggly, so small and whole. He's like the final inside nesting doll, the one you can't take apart.

When Amy returned, she announced that she and Jax were going back to Chicago in a couple of weeks. The elevator dropped inside me. "Oh, just for ten days," she said.

April 22
God has apparently had it with subtlety and nuance, because now I have laryngitis. So the day after Amy told me about her next trip to Chicago, I lost my voice.

As I was stewing this afternoon about her trip and my infirmity, Sam came by to get some money for art supplies. I couldn't even inflict my goodness on him, because I had neither voice nor energy. He seemed to be doing well. He stretched out on the couch and put on a baseball game. After a while he got up to go to the kitchen, and when he passed me, long-legged and fatherly — proud and humbled at the same time — I asked hoarsely, "Are you okay with Amy and Jax leaving again?"

He shrugged and said, "And my choices would be?" He turned up his palms. Then he reached down to pat me on the top of my head. Next thing I know, he will be pretending to pull off the tip of my nose and displaying the end of his thumb from behind his fingers. I had to laugh, although it hurt my throat. When I get wobbly from umbrage, it can be quantum: everyone in the family universe gets wobbly. I make a bad matriarch, what with my bad nerves and tiny opinions.

When he came back, he listened to the baseball game while I lay on the smaller couch and read. Then he turned off the TV, and made some sketches in his notebook for quite a while.

Silence is an extension of music. It is the spaciousness that is deep within, that expresses and is complete each moment as it lolls about, or spirals out and back in like a fiddlehead fern, and I got to be with my son in this silence, except for the scritch-scratch of his pencil on the paper.

Sometimes I look at this handsome young man lost in study, his long limbs and huge brown eyes, and I forget he has a baby at home.

The silence has been good for me today — not talking has subdued the rackety noise of fear in my head. I filled the silence with things that nourish me, instead of stuff that tears me down. I took naps with the animals, picked flowers from the garden — lilies and daisies — had tea and vanilla ice cream. I rested all day on the couch with a book, then made a quiet old-lady dinner of lentil soup and more ice cream. I felt much better afterward, like my regular old self again, which is to say good, with an underlying thrum of dread.

April 24
Tom called from the airport, waiting for a flight to Australia. He was in a bad mood, although he will never admit this. We both have close friends in dire health, and friends with kids who are profoundly sick.

We talked for a while about how our various friends were doing, and then I asked if I could pose a theological question, and he sighed deeply, although I know he loves that I question so much. I asked him: If — as he had once explained — God is the Lover, Jesus the Beloved, and the Holy Spirit the animating love between them, then where does Mary fit in?

"Mary is also loved. But she is not the Source. The Trinity is. The Trinity is the dance, and Mary invites us all to the dance floor, and she opens the door. She welcomes everyone to come in to the dance."

"Like the opposite of a bouncer."

"That's right. She is loved, she is Love. But she's not foundational. Now, we don't like to mention this to you and your little feminist friends, because it sounds a tiny bit harsh, and all of you take it the wrong way, boo-hoo, boo-hoo. But you have to have a penis to be the Source."

Laughter lifts the phonograph needle out of the scratches on my heart's album. When I was a child, I knew that something scary or weird could happen at any time, because it did. Without laughter, I skip straight to this old scratch. It's deep, and you'd better be prepared for things to go bad.

April 25

Some of the same old-lady baby-snatchers who fought over Sam twenty years ago came after Jax today at church. "Give me that baby." "It's my turn." I perfectly remember two of our saints, Zerline and Mary Williams, hissing at each other, underneath the sermon: "You're *hoggin'* that baby."

The first Scripture reading today was Luke 15, the Prodigal Son. Of course. It's the only real story — coming back to God, who welcomes us with heartbroken joy, no matter what, every time. I do not get this.

The plainness of the church is restful. I relaxed, as I always do here, because everyone was down-to-earth, joining in the most ordinary of human things to do, singing together, handing one another Kleenex, grabbing for the babies. Spirit gets on you at this joint like a light drizzle, making you look up and take notice.

When Jax fussed, I walked and jostled him in the back of the church, which is thirty feet from the front. During a lull, I stopped to tell the older, gorgeous Iraqi wife of a retired African-American minister how beautiful she looked in the rich purples and maroons she was wearing, and she said, "You look beautiful in that grandson."

April 26
Jax spent the morning in my living room, shouting as he bounced up and down in his bouncy saucer, an easy ten minutes at a stretch with his strong thigh muscles, playing all the different gears and whistles. He was like a one-man band, Dick Van Dyke in *Mary Poppins.*

I look at him and think, Who is the big kid coiled up in there, the teenager who is going to scare Amy and Sam to death? I think of Sam's friends who still live in town, the kids at my church who've gotten lost and even died, a relative's fourteen-year-old daughter who is in an institution for eating disorders. They're like those firework snakes of dark ash that uncoil when you light the tablets. These lost, hurting children uncoiled from the babies they were: joyous, adored. Now they've broken their parents' hearts.

As a baby, Sam was not as loud as Jax is;

he was a little shy, always watchful, searching for clues about people and the world. I
was an anxious and confused mother, struggling to make ends meet, and with a best
friend who was diagnosed with metastatic
breast cancer when Sam was seven months
old. Also, there was no father around.
Maybe as a result Sam was more deliberate,
more cautious in his exploration of the
world, whereas Jax is utterly mellow and
spontaneous. He moves from his own center, while Sam was more dependent on me:
how I was doing, how I was coping. I had
done this semi-insane thing, having a child
at an extra-stressful age in life, with no
money — which Sam and Amy have done,
too — and for financial reasons I was stuck
living in a dark and peculiar house with no
light. Amy and Sam are too, but they can
come here whenever they want, where there
are six skylights, and lots of room. And their
parents pay all the bills.

I had an informal co-op while raising Sam:
his godmothers Pammy and Peggy, grandmothers Nikki and Gertrud, Stevo, Sam's
makeshift Big Brother Brian, Bill and
Emmy, Millard, Neshama, four adopted and
cherished gay uncles. I borrowed the rent
from friends when I needed to. Some of
them bought me a washing machine. Sam

was playful, watchful, curious, filled with scientific wonder, a sweet, silly boy, too, but quieter than his son. Jax is louder joy, lifting, flinging, uncovering, discovering, bouncing up and down. I don't think the world was quite as safe for Sam as it is for Jax, and this makes me feel terrible. But I'm glad beyond words that, because of the co-op's great work, Jax has a father around.

April 27
Spring gets you every time. Every year it sucks me in, but then, I'm easy — a few cool blue skies, new grass, wildflowers, and I'm in love. You're going to fall for that old magic trick again? Oh, yeah.

Today our green hills look like they need a haircut. There are daffodils sprouting, narcissus (and the smaller version, paper whites) among the grass and weeds. The way the spring light falls on blades of grass can undo me. Of course, coiled up in all this beauty is horrible summer. The spring is bait, like babyhood. It's how life keeps you hooked in. Just as the endless cold and rain start to gain the upper hand in the war for your spirit, spring comes out to hike up its skirts and seduce you.

Spring comes infinitely more quickly and often, the older you get, seemingly every seven months now. The faster the merry-go-round spins, the more blurry it gets, and the Viennese music begins to sound a little warped.

Everything is so lovely against the green — flowers and white egrets in the meadows, horses and cows in the fields lining the road on the way to the coast. The cows are the color of See's lollypops. The sky is oceanic blue. You would need a lot of weaverly tricks to capture the spectrum of blue, from the bright baby blue of eyes, to pale blue, all the way to eggshell and white.

In summer, you just walk around making sounds like Lurch.

April 28, E-mail from Mary T
A young friend of mine from church, who's now also close to Amy, took care of Jax. She e-mailed me this morning.

"Hi Annie: I loved babysitting Jax. We observed big kids at the park, two and three year olds and he sort of made friends with a seven-month-old named Chloe in the baby swings. She smiled at him the whole time and he just looked at her so seriously and didn't take his eyes off her once, not even to blink.

"Later we were at the grassy dog park in Fairfax when a baby squirrel fell from the sky and landed on a woman's lap. We think a big bird must have dropped it because the woman wasn't under a tree. It was healthy looking and very tiny. Jax made such funny faces when he saw it. Initially, when he first spotted it, he did a bit of a double take, and looked at the squirrel with big eyes, then looked at me with a half-smile, then back at the squirrel. This is what the expression was on his face for most of the dramatic squirrel experience: what the FUCK?

"The face he made gave me the impression that he thought it was somewhat pathetic, like he knew he was much bigger and more important than this squirrel, but he was still curious about it. The woman who had it fall on her lap walked around with the authority of Mother Goose, and the baby squirrel followed her around everywhere, hopping like a bunny because it seemed to have a broken back leg. Jax's mouth was hanging wide open at this time and he made eye contact with me a few times to see what I thought. The woman would stop and kneel by the squirrel and stroke its back with a tiny stick, and the squirrel would close his eyes in bliss, with his butt up in the air and face burrowed in the grass while she did this. Then it would get back to following her around the park.

We were still there when the animal rescue van from the Humane Society came to take him to the hospital."

May 2
Amy and Jax left for Chicago a few days ago.

This morning I went for a hike in the hills with the dogs. I brought Jax up here in his baby backpack last week. I won't be able to carry him much longer. My back ached almost as soon as we started, and we had to stop often. Right below us was the yard of the school where Sam went for fourth and fifth grade, and around it, a very organized, rich-pink ring of plum trees was in full bloom, with a green doily of leaves holding it all up. It was crazy, like Bozo's head or a circle of giant manicured poodles. It must have been a full plum orchard back in the day. Maybe it's a landing strip for Alturians now. It's as beautiful and intense as the stained glass at Mission Dolores.

I loved the weightlessness of not having Jax on my back. Today the blossoms were fully opened, mauve, silver, and cool pink.

May 6, Another E-mail Field Report from Mary T
My friend Mary e-mailed me again:

"Dear Annie: you asked for more details on my day with Jax. After the incident with the squirrel who fell from the sky, we went to the other park, where all the swings and older kids are. His face was just as rapt with the big kids at the park, as it was with the squirrel. I took him up close up to observe them at the climbing structure. Some of the kids gave me dirty looks because we were really up in their business, but Jax and I were very brave and stayed put. When Jax looked at the squirrel, he knew that he was bigger and cooler than it was; when he observed the big kids, he knew they were bigger, and he thought they were so cool. The seven-month-old girl, Chloe, had *no* teeth showing, she was all gums and smiles, with such a big mouth and a shiny bald head. She looked like my grandpa Earl, only uglier. I loved her, such a happy funny-looking baby girl. Jax didn't smile at her once, even though that's all she did for him."

May 9

It is Mother's Day. Amy and Jax are still in Chicago. They are having brunch with Trudy at the grandmother's convalescent home; they don't get back until late this afternoon, so Neshama and I picked Sam up at ten and drove to Los Altos.

There were only four people there when we arrived, and horribly, no Ragu, who is the main reason we come. Also, the nice elderly Jewish-looking harmonium player was not there. Instead, there was a beautiful, overweight Deadhead type playing guitar and chant-singing *Baba nam kevalam,* and two young Asian women doing light harmonies. It felt nice and familiar and harmonic, like Peter, Paul & Mary during their early years. The guitar made you feel bouncier in the body than the harmonium did. The quality of the harmonium is sharp and wheezy, and otherworldly, whereas this guitar was *quite* worldly.

The young women were lovely and light, eyes closed dreamily.

I found it distressing that the ancient harmonium player was not there, but then he arrived, and went to the back of the room to take his place among the other latecomers. In front, the emaciated Indian man leading today's service was dressed in saffron robes, and I did not feel any real contact with him. I thought of him as the Sub, like some math substitute who has to fill in for a history teacher. He was shifting vaguely from foot to foot, gently removed from us, like someone who had dropped in from another plane of existence, like Jax's squirrel. He didn't do it right, like we are big experts now.

Sam stood beside me in his most private stance. Watching someone in devotion is more private than watching someone sleep, which is so paradoxical, like most truth, since you see a person's deepest interior landscape in community. This place is great because you get to mess up, to lose your balance a little, lose rhythm, get out of sync, and still be okay. I almost had to pinch myself that the three of us were all together here, on Mother's Day, doing this for the experience of it, even though we didn't have a clue, really, what the experience was. Except that we were moving in the same rhythm, in a room where everyone had opened up to being together in the cluelessness, and in kindness. That doesn't happen very often in our regular worlds.

Orange is a dominant color here and in India, vibrant, rich, and juicy, the color of the mangoes Indians love so much. It's hot and bright, although you'd think they'd get enough hot and bright in India.

Here at the ashram, we had this ecstatic connection with that rare and elusive Orangeness, something bigger than ourselves, embodied in the ancient chants, and the side-to-side, and the soft, soft kindness.

The devotion of swaying from foot to foot is knowing that in life, we're always shifting, and sometimes we can do it with a modicum of intention and planted harmony. Holding the two-footed stance was very tiring. I remembered (it being Mother's Day) how many millions of hours I have swayed from side to side holding baby Sam and now baby Jax.

Chanting, you join your strand to everyone else's, to the weave of the whole group. This must be what heaven is like, along with laughter and an excellent dessert table. *Baba nam kevalam,* love is all there is.

We moved on to the velvety silence of meditation time. Some silences are hollow, or many-layered, like echoes. But this one is slightly furry and inviting. You could drink it down. And when Ragu arrived during meditation, my heart skipped. He's a Love rock star.

Even though he tiptoed in, he managed to make a sloshy, swampy, big-loud-engine arrival. I always forget how dark he is — and more than anyone I've seen, he looks like pure love, like God in a denim jacket.

The Sub, on the other hand, seemed spectral, compared with Ragu, as if he had risen from a gurney. Or maybe orange just wasn't his color.

Ragu looked like a cheerful shopkeeper, very much at home in this world. The lower voices of the men, chanting — Ragu, Sam, the Sub, the regular harmonium player, who was still in the back — were like bellows, while those of the women, the Asian women and Neshama, were clear, as if they came out of a pure, thin water pipe, and they spread like a glaze over the other voices and sounds.

Sam was centered and quietly happy on the way home. He said:

"I want to tell you two things I got from you. One is that my first response is usually to make sure I am not doing anything wrong, or anything that stands out or is offensive. I hate this. The other thing is that I am able to enter an experience, and love it, and get it, and find myself surrounded by the least likely angels. I always saw you do that, even when I was a little kid. Like now, I can see you being friends and laughing with Tea Party people, or bikers."

Mother's Day is my new favorite holiday.

Sam said he liked that the guitarist sounded so mortal. "He had a cold, like I might, and was quietly hacking and rasping and coughing, but he still led us, some regular person. I guess I get liking this from you, too."

May 10, Interview with Sam

"Hi, Mom. I really wanted to cancel yesterday because I had so many sketches due, and wanted to get the house ready for Amy, but I knew there was no hope for me, because it was Mother's Day and you'd been urgently reminding me for days, and were, let's say, in some sort of state, about wanting me to go with you.

"I had so much inner resistance, till the very second we stepped through the door where kirtan is held. I even took my shoes off at the front door in this deep resistance. But as soon as I got into the room, by the third sway from side to side, I was totally disarmed. Swaying from side to side gave me my balance back, and that helped, so I knew I could work effectively on my homework later. It happened instantly — or in three steps, anyway. You correct your physical balance a lot of times here, like, Oops, I stepped too far over, or too slowly — okay, now I'm back, and happy, and free, because I'm balanced.

"The last time I was in Chicago with Amy, we had a fight, and we decided to go our separate ways, so she drove off with Jax, and I was downtown, without a clue where I was. But by the time she came back for me, half an hour later, I'd made friends with all

275

these scary penitentiary types, black and white, and they were hanging together, laughing, and they had become my guardian angels. I got this from you, and I appreciate it."

May 11
Amy is back, and the mood is tense and stressful, because she had to leave her best friends and relatives behind again. I was trying to *Baba nam* it, but the fact is, Amy does not want to live here. Nothing I do changes this. My blinkered, cheerful vision and armored habits are not helpful. I do not know how to get with what I know to be true, that life is change, and that we need muscle, flexibility, and awareness. Unfortunately, these are not my strong suits. My strong suits are held breath and false good cheer.

Jax, on the other hand, makes me laugh just by virtue of his being a baby, a radiant love being. Maybe we all are — Amy, Sam, and even I, inside these fat suits of personality and protection. I know we were once. It's a little harder to see in people over the age of four.

Today was hard, or at least a mixed grill. There is the loveliness of people at the ashram, and the spring, both of which convince me that everything comes from God, even we do: Tom said once that in incarnation God enters into everything, and I can see that. Yet at the same time, there is the nightmare of other people, both their damage and their having such influence in my life. In spring, in Resurrection, everything comes back to life, theoretically. In my thinking, it all dies. Perhaps this is something I should take a look at.

May 13

John Muir once said that to see the face of God, you do not need to open a book or go to church or temple; you have only to go to Yosemite. And you are part of the world's beauty. God, and the beauty of God's creation, and you complete a circuit. I am not sure that my parents remembered to mention this to me. But I told Sam, and he believes it, and will tell Jax.

I would say that my deepest spiritual understanding is that God also sees and forgives my smallest detail, even my flickery, prickly, damaged, jealous, vain self, and sees how I get self-righteous and feel either like trash, often, or superior, and like such a scaredy-cat, and God still understands exactly what that feels like. Because God has had the experience of being people, through Jesus.

Jesus had his good days and bad days and stomach viruses. Not to mention that on top of it all, he had a *mom* who had bad days and good days of her own. She's like me and Amy, like all of us; she would have been as hormonal, too. And she must have been jealous sometimes of the people Jesus chose to spend time with instead of her. Jealousy is such a toxic virus. "Who *are* these people? And what do they have that I don't have?" It's pretty easy to be deeply selfish when it comes to sharing your child. Even Mary must have been like: "Back off! He's *mine.*"

May 16

Amy brought Jax into church late, sound asleep in his car seat, and he stayed asleep in the rhythmic burble of the prayers and the first hymn. Then, at the second hymn, "What a Friend We Have in Jesus," one of our members began to accompany us on her exotic Korean drum — how had I not noticed her up by the choir? Bam, bash, like rifle fire, a funeral salute — *Crash! Crack! Blam!* Jax bolted awake in Foster Brooks mode, and looked around. I had to force myself not to glare at her for waking the baby. Jax's eyes landed on Amy's, then mine, then back on Amy's. Then he dropped back to sleep.

He'll be ten months old in a few days. He is a full participant in human life, except when, as today, he has been drinking. He has all sorts of human skills and desires, like being able to focus on things for as long as he chooses, talking away with a thoughtful expression even as he makes farting, spluttering noises. He also wants things now, and holds on — our two most human tendencies: he needs and grasps everything within his range, and doesn't immediately lose interest in something if he can't have instant gratification.

When he woke up for real, we took him out of his car seat so he could look around. Danielle, my hairdresser, held him for a long time. She is very large, and fully tattooed to her neck, with her arms, her cleavage, her everything brilliantly decorated in flowers and hearts of all sizes, and Jesus and sunrises — her entire retirement fund seemingly spent on these designs. Jax stared, just a few inches from each body painting, touching them carefully as if he could trace them, which he can't quite yet, and gaping as if at an IMAX movie screen, stoned.

During the sermon, our guest preacher, Laurie, asked from the pulpit, "What do we do when we are at our most scared and lonely, feeling overwhelmed and misunderstood, guilty and abandoned?"

There was a long pause.

Then someone ventured: "Eat?"

May 19

Amy left Jax with me for the whole day. I loved it, but as usual was wiped out by the time she returned. Luckily, I have a gift for getting him to take naps with me. We took two, one in the late morning, one mid-afternoon. I hold him, swaying, and sing him Jesus or union songs until he drops off. Then I curl up with him on the couch, with him tucked into my armpit, between the couch and my side, both of us under a baby blanket.

May 20

I went hiking with Karen early this morning, up in the hills with the dogs. In late spring, the land in these parts is covered with a great fleece quilt like a landscape weaving, with clumps of interesting textures, feathery Asian touches, lots of broccoli trees, infinite poppies, buttercups like buttons securing it all. There are shades of purple-brown and orange in all the green, in the trees and the grass, and heathery rose, colors you don't see except in paintings, like someone up here is spinning and dyeing her own yarn.

It's Wordsworth up here, the glint of an infinite field of benevolence.

Karen lets me catch her up on Jax for the first ten minutes of every weekly walk now. It can't be very interesting. I used to hate new grandmothers. I told her about Jax lifting his knees off the ground to walk, how brilliant he is to pay attention to his pain-avoidance instincts — something I don't always do anymore, especially when it comes to men.

He's figured out that when you can't find things, they might still be there: if you cover up an apple with a hat, he now lifts the hat, and by God, there's that damn apple! But I feel a recurrent bittersweet sadness in realizing what's in store for him — what a mishmash of surprise and joy, tedium and desolation this life will bring.

Nature is the greatest solace.

Karen, who is five years younger than I am, has had a physical ache in her heart for a week, and is going in for a day of heart tests this afternoon. I asked whether we should even be hiking. She thought I was crazy. What if this is her last day on earth? She wants to have hiked; I want to have had dessert. She says she wants to get a tattoo on her chest that says "Do Not Resuscitate." But she is not a grandmother yet.

May 20
We had a Cousins lunch today, with Clara, Jax, Stevo, and Amy, to celebrate Jax's ten-month birthday. Sam was in school. Stevo and Annette are getting married in ten days. It is a great happiness for our family, right up there with having Jax join us; and we are sad only that Millard didn't live long enough to celebrate with us. There are gaping holes in everything. Life is a nice fresh batch of Swiss cheese. (Note to self: Savor the holes, too, like the spaces between musical notes.) I am the officiant, Sam will be Stevo's best man, Clara will walk her dad down the aisle of redwoods behind the restaurant, and Jax will steal the show.

Jax is so together now that he could be in the wedding party. He's a total smiling charmer, mastering new skills every day. Really, he'll be working the fax machine soon. All smiles, drool, focus, grabbing, and motion. Whenever he's on his stomach, he does a workout routine that would have put Jack LaLanne to shame, a hybrid of push-ups, with a mad stationary dash. It's exhausting to watch.

Today we were hanging out in the sun with the dogs. Jax, wearing just a diaper, started crawling around like Speedy Gonzales and then realized the concrete was hurting his knees. So he straightened his legs and got around on his hands and the bottoms of his feet. Lily was stunned — it apparently turns out that the baby unit is *not* a badger, as previously thought, but a primate of some sort. *Proconsul africanus. Australopithecus. Ecce Homo!*

May 21

I met Amy, Sam, and Jax at Fort Mason, the presidio near the southern base of the Golden Gate Bridge. A friend of Sam's who is a professional photographer had offered to take their photos, and I got to be a part of the process. I could tell Sam and Amy had had a bad morning — he was at his most petulant when they arrived, and she was in enraged-victim mode. They managed to pull out of it somewhat as Sam's friend and her assistant herded us from backdrop to backdrop — in front of various buildings, statues, and the Bay. I watched the woman photograph Jax on Sam's shoulders, and with the sea shimmering behind them, I fixated on the specter of Amy's taking Jax to Chicago. My thoughts careened off one another like bumper cars: happy thoughts about the beauty of the day and the blessing of Jax; thoughts about how to bribe Sam into behaving better with Amy, and how to get Amy to be nicer to Sam; images of me drowning in the frigid bay, and being eaten by a great white shark out by the Farollon Islands.

Then, out of nowhere, I remembered something a man named Bob Earle said years ago: that his mind wanted to kill him and try to live on its own. And in a blink my bad trance was broken. I said to my mind, "You can't have me," and then said to God, "Do resuscitate, *do*," and the wind blew, the gulls cried, and Jax laughed. I stopped thinking about trying to fix and rescue Sam and Amy; and much more important, I stopped talking. I was revived.

As she worked, the photographer said how great the pictures of this day were going to be, and this surprised Sam and Amy. They both rose to the taxing occasion, and the beauty of the setting — the pelicans; the jewel that is a former prison, Alcatraz; the macramé Golden Gate Bridge.

They were being friendlier to each other when they left. Jax was learning to wave bye-bye, which added ten minutes to our windy farewell.

May 25

I have a fabulous beautiful vintage dress from the fifties that I always wear when I perform weddings. It's soft rose, with cap sleeves, a scooped neckline, lots of shimmering pink sequins, and side zippers from the waist to the armpits.

I went to get it out yesterday, for Stevo's wedding to Annette, this Sunday — and it had shrunk in the closet. I hate when this happens. I could zip it up when I put it on, although the zipper kept trapping and pinching bits of rib-cage fat. Amy was watching me try it on, and laughing. There's tummy there that (I like to think) looks sort of adorable when covered with a T-shirt or jammies, but it's not quite as cute when bulging into a tight sequined bodice.

I did get the dress on and the zippers zipped, but barely. I haven't lost my grandbaby fat. Also, what happens in a dark closet, where there is no air circulating, is that the fabric can't breathe, and it dies a little every day. It atrophies and contracts, like old apples or balloons. I'm certain of it.

You can take items suffering from closet shrink to be altered, or you can starve yourself. Or you can do what every woman in her right mind does: buy a tubular latex girdle containment product for the gut.

Which is what I did that afternoon. I bought some Spanx.

May 25, Interview with Sam

Sam and Jax came over for a couple of hours. Sam was lovely and relaxed, and we ate vast quantities of corn chips, salsa, and carrot cake together, since Spanx has solved all my imminent problems. Jax race-crawled around the house, stopping to study and drop things, manhandle the animals, and smash up bites of banana on the table before shoving them into his mouth. He's Koko the gorilla gone bad.

Sam gave him his bottle, and rocked him to sleep in his arms, as casual as can be, and it filled me with a crushing love, something like pain, and with pride, the way I felt when other kids fell in love with my father.

I asked Sam, "How would you describe Jax to someone who's never met him?"

Sam said, "I'd say he is an intellectual."

"Jax?"

"Oh, yeah, he's a thinker, but a cool guy, not a nerd. He is just like his dad — he can't leave something alone until he understands it."

"How would you describe him physically?"

"He's a strong yet softly rounded boy. He's a lunk, very powerful in his own thinky way. He's golden olive-brown — he has the color skin every white person wants."

"Tell me about his sense of humor."

"He likes candid situations — he's not going to laugh at what you think is funny. He loves spontaneous things, and sight gags. The funniest thing on earth to him is anyone sneezing, including himself. He just loses his mind laughing."

"How would you say you and I are most different?"

"Well, you're more fearful. You need a lot more things to be in place for you to feel safe. But you did not get hit by the lavish thing. I definitely have the lavish thing. I want to own a lot of great shit. You don't have this — I mean, look at your old car. I guess where we're most different is that you're very simple."

My mouth dropped open. I hadn't seen that coming: *me,* a simpleton.

Then he added, "No offense."

May 26

It is devastating to watch the second month of BP's catastrophic oil spill in the Gulf of Mexico. There is apparently nothing anyone can do, not even Obama. The whole country feels a collective, agitated despair.

I don't see how God can turn this tragedy around. He didn't send me the e-mail yet. This is always a difficult decision for Him: "Hmmmm, let's see — should I send Annie the briefing and get her *always* excellent ideas and input? Or should I just call it a day?"

I wish I could see the hand of God more clearly. Tom says I am one of those people who run after Jesus going, "Give us a sign, Lord, give us a sign." So He gives me a sign — and then two days later I'm running after him again, crying, "Show me another sign." Tom says this is why I am on God's special list: I've gotten endless signs of the greatness of God's love and hilarious care, but I always end up needing a newer sign, maybe one that is cuter and more spangly.

May 31
The day finally arrived. It was sunny and warm for the wedding yesterday under the redwoods at Deer Park. Annette's daughter Rachel and the other maids of honor led the procession down the aisle past one hundred or so beloved friends and relatives. Sam was next. Clara and I walked Stevo down the aisle. Stevo looked like our father, tall and handsome, blue-eyed, with dark

wavy hair and a long nose. Our older brother, John, looks more like Mom, darker and sturdier, brown-eyed, with a smaller nose. His health has been poor for the last few years; he is very religious, and involved with his church in Chico, so he definitely had that radiant love thing going. All three of us got clean and sober twenty-plus years ago, and we are all believers, which must leave our parents scratching their heads in the grave or in heaven, and wondering, "Where did we go wrong?" It is actually a miracle that we are still alive, all things considered. And it felt like that today, especially, I might add, because I hadn't even needed to wear the Spanx — talk about cute signs from God. This was like Lourdes.

Most of our cousins were there, and Sam's two cousins: John's teenage son, Tyler, who is half Japanese-American; and Clara at her most gorgeous in lace and little heels, with flowers in her hair.

Jax looked like a drunken Cuban band-leader in a black-and-white vest, a white dress shirt, black shorts, and black bow tie. Amy wore the sexiest sleeveless clingy blue dress.

I said what I always say at weddings: That two people fall in love and decide to see if their love might stand up over time; if there might be enough grace and forgiveness and the occasional memory lapse to hold their love together into the fullness of time. That we celebrate the commitment to this work, to the joy, to the inevitable struggles, to the energy that is both sweet and deep that the two people exude in their love for each other. That we celebrate our senses of humor and patience, and the greatness and cost of enduring family love.

Annette and Sam cried during the ceremony. Birds sang. Jax sat in Amy's lap in the front row and made farting noises, and clapped.

The sweetest moment in the glorious binge of a reception was when Sam toasted the couple, and everyone cried except me, with my cold stone heart; Sam said Stevo was the closest he'd had to a father while growing up, and that Stevo was the best adoptive dad both he and Clara ever could have had — neither of them needed a birth dad, after they were born, since they had Stevo. No dad could have been funnier, Sam said, or played more on the floor with them, and he'd done such a great job with helping them both with Legos, and homework, and helping them have a great sense of humor, and taking them to Giants games.

He said no one in the family would ever think anyone was good enough for Stevo, but finally, in Annette, we were convinced that someone was.

Stevo and Annette's first dance was to Roberta Flack singing "The First Time Ever I Saw Your Face," and after they had a moment alone on the floor, five perfect Marin married couples joined in. I felt a little spinstery, but it was hard not to feel great in a tight-fitting rose-colored dress with sequins, and Jax in my arms, in his Cuban-bandleader vest and bow tie, taking it all in. He and I danced twice, to "Hot Stuff" and "On the Street Where You Live." Then he passed out, so we sat under a redwood tree and I held court, as my queenly English mother used to do.

June 2
Sam had a great line over the phone today. I had asked that he write up his version of the wedding, and I called to see how it was coming along. He said fine; he was nearly done. I told him to be sure to mention how thin and cute I looked in my vintage rose dress, and there was a pause. Then he said, "Mom, will you mind very much if you are not the main subject of my piece about Stevo's wedding?"

It was clear my uncle Stevo's wedding was officially under way when I got a typical call from my mother, just over a week before the wedding.

Mom: "Hi, it's Worried Mommy."

Me: "Hi, Mommy, what can I do for you?"

Mom: "I'm worried that you keep putting off getting your measurements at the tuxedo store. Stevo's wedding is only nine days away. Please don't let him down. It's a great honor to be his best man."

Me: "Oh, this isn't Worried Mom. This is Guilt-Mongering Mom. I promise I'll take care of it. You have nothing to worry about."

She had real reason to be concerned. This was the most important assignment of my life, after fatherhood. That's how much I love Stevo. But I have zero free time to do anything besides school and Jax.

The day of the wedding rehearsal I made sure to stop by the suit store (whose name we will not mention until the check clears) to make sure that my suit fit. The suit was fine, so I called Uncle to let him know we didn't have to cancel the wedding on my behalf. From the store I drove down to Mom's, where people were gathered for the rehearsal. Walking into my mother's house, the overall mood and fashion were so casual

I don't think a stranger looking in would have had the slightest hint that a wedding was a day away. When I was a kid, I desperately wanted us to be a more normal family — like have china, and dress up more, and have professional photographers take our pictures every Christmas. My mother's idea of formal was to put our food on plates. Now I see we were great, but kind of odd — and you don't want to be odd when you're young.

We all made our way down to the location of the wedding, which was in the huge backyard of a restaurant right around the corner from my Mom's, and completely bare, with no indications of how it would be decorated and transformed. I tried squinting to imagine what they were going to do with the place. To keep us on our toes, the actual wedding planner was not there to instruct us. Oh, well. Instead, one of Annette's friends stood in and whipped us into shape. She was actually pretty cool, and saved the day. The instructions were easy, though — only two things to remember. One was the order in which we walked down the aisle, and two was to wait twenty seconds between each person. But at the actual wedding not one of us got it right. We are sort of a funny family that way. Neshama's husband used to say at family gatherings, "We're a bum outfit." Ching ching.

Later, we had a great Puerto Rican takeout banquet at my mother's: chicken backs, rice, beans, plantains, enough for a hundred instead of the twenty of us who were there. Then, two hours after this party begins, my mom says to everyone enthusiastically, "Okay, time to go home now." She does this pretty routinely, on holidays and our birthdays. The funny thing is, everyone is always really relieved, although I still find it slightly embarrassing.

The day of the wedding, Amy, Jax and I showed up at my mom's very early. Her small, quiet house had been transformed into a World War II factory run by women, a fully functioning in-house operation with various stations set up. Jax and I sat outside in the backyard to kill some time and just be together before the craziness started. Half an hour later, Uncle walked up and said, "It's getting time to get the suits on," so we decided to suit up away from everyone else, in the garage that my mom likes to pretend is her pool house. The time we spent was a true best-man-and-groom moment; I will never forget it. I am very honored to have been there for one of my role models in life. I got to get his suit for him from inside the house, and we talked about how great he felt and what a blessed guy he was, and about funny moments we had spent together over the last twenty years. We wanted a snack, and we discussed whether we should go inside, because in the old days you weren't supposed to see your bride until the wedding. He said, "Oh no, we're old, it's our second wedding. It doesn't matter." So we walked inside and instantly got yelled at by the women: "STEVO, GET OUT!" Clara got to be one of the women, even though she's only seven, and was fussed over by the hair-and-makeup friend — she was the happiest, most beautiful girl, in a great lacy white dress and big-girl heels, to walk her dad down the aisle. This just about broke my heart with happiness.

Stevo really wanted to walk to his wedding, and (even though I didn't) we headed off with Jax in his stroller, so he didn't drool all over my tux. We walked slowly down the road to the back of the restaurant, to the spot underneath the redwoods, and luxuriously took everything in. It was like being in a mini Muir Woods.

The restaurant had transformed the space into a real summer wedding site, like in the movies, with flowers and ribbons and lanterns, and garlands tying together the redwood trees. When the groomsmen arrived shortly after we got there, the wedding planner directed us to the bar-and-deck area. Back there we drank water, got our big Mafia flower corsages on our suits, and talked. I was reminded what great friends my uncle has, all of them sober like him — and how amazing that he picked me out of all of his friends to be his best man. That's when my mind went blank with the pressure of trying not to screw up — I was so excited the wedding was starting that right in front of everyone, all one hundred people, I spaced out, and crashed like a drunk into the groomsman ahead of me; luckily, there was no domino effect.

Except for Jax's birth, it was probably the happiest day of my life.

June 7

Everyone — the newlyweds, Amy, Sam, Jax — came to my house after church yesterday, for no particular reason, except that the wedding last Sunday was so lovely that I suggested Stevo and Annette come over and renew their vows. We ate huge amounts of lasagna, salad, chocolate-covered strawberries. Sometimes — like at weddings or funerals — you have to eat vast quantities because you need to be weighted. You need ballast, or you might just float away in the pain or joy or anxiety. Other times, like today, you just want to shovel it in, for fun, and because you don't want to have to think too much. Eating is so familiar, and marvelously stupid.

I took care of Jax while Sam and Amy went to the movies, and for the first time when he woke up from his nap, he was not crying to be picked up; instead, he just squawked once from the crib, loudly, like a bitter chicken. When I came into the room, he stood gripping the bars of his portable crib, looking like an inmate about two minutes from calling his prison advocacy rep.

June 9

Tomorrow I am flying to Chicago to stay with Doug for a few days and to give a talk at a book festival. Amy has arranged for several relatives and friends to attend. She wants us all to know one another, because we are very important to her and Jax — one big happy family, et cetera. I pretend to think and want this, too, but I secretly hope that instead they will see what a fabulous person I am, and will not want Amy to take

Jax away from me. They'll see what a tragedy it would be to deprive Jax of my influence for more than, say, two weeks at a stretch, and even that might be stretching it. Amy showed me their pictures on Facebook, her friends, cousins, grandma. She adores them: they're the people she has loved most deeply all her life. I feel slightly competitive with them, which I hate in myself — but we on the West Coast have had less than three years to convince Amy of our excellence, while they've had years and even lifetimes to strut their stuff. Still, I see how ridiculous my jealousy is, and am seriously starting to think I have problems sharing.

Amy left Jax with me for a few hours. He was a hurricane of destruction and good cheer. When he crawls away from a room, he leaves it looking like a frat house. Every single book on low-lying shelves must be flung to the floor. Also — this is new — he seems to be in a workshop on the concept of In and Out, and Off. Everything must get flung over the side of everything else: All the books on any shelves he can reach, Off. All of Clara's pony figurines in their box, Out. Then they all go back In. Then Out again. It's dizzying. He's wired and methodical in his work, like a tiny German crackhead.

June 13

A three-day weekend with Doug in Chicago, where I was speaking at the *Tribune* Lit Fest. A weekend of rain and the threat of thunderstorms, and then sun flickered through and there was blue sky again and the day turned warm, and then black clouds returned. Doug and I spent hours at Millennium Park, where musicians were playing every kind of music around every leafy, brilliantly landscaped corner. Most nights of the summer, there are outdoor concerts in the park, and you walk beneath the gigantic, fantastic silver mirrored "Bean," like a spaceship hovering ten feet off the ground, to see yourself in crazy fun-house reflection and perspective from all sides and fields of it. There are fountains for kids and babies to splash and cool off in. There was a Matisse exhibition at the Art Institute, where I copied down the notes on one painting, which had the phrase "radical becoming." That stopped me in my tracks. They were the words of the philosopher Henri Bergson, "reality as a state of radical becoming, constant flux, graspable only by intuition." Rattly rides on the El, and theater on bus rides filled with Anna Deavere Smith characters. Sunday morning we took the El to Doug's church, which is much like St.

Andrew in terms of intergenerational and multiethnic peace and justice passion and mission outreach, with a black associate pastor, a rousing choir, and a sermon identifying where Jesus' message butts up against white privilege, male and straight privilege. I realized that Sam would love this place. Ack! Ack! Please, God, if You love me, shoot me now.

And a couple of hours later, I experienced a true-blue epiphany in Doug's guest room, while packing my bags. I had the full-body conviction — after twenty months of feeling terrorized by the very thought — that it would be okay if Amy and Jax, or Amy and Sam and Jax, moved to Chicago. It would be okay. I would be okay. It would be fantastic for Sam to live in this great city, and maybe go to the Art Institute here. Jax, Doug, and I could splash around in the fountains with Chicago jazz playing behind us, and string quartets. Sure, maybe I would cry at first and go into withdrawal, and have a nervous breakdown; but then I would come through.

June 14
Well, that was fun while it lasted.

Now I must think of new ways to persuade Amy to want to live in California. Must help her get some great friends. Or here's a good idea: get her relatives and best Chicago friends to move here. They can all live with me. And I'll help them get great jobs, including the grandmother; she can work at one of the local Catholic thrift shops.

Still, a knot inside me is releasing ever so slightly. I continue to feel powerless and doomed, but in a slightly more relaxed way.

June 15

Sam, Amy, and Jax were here today for hamburgers and inedible hippie fries. It was a warm afternoon, the three of them sweet and lovely together. Amy was at her most easygoing, and I felt that we were working out a seriously touching mother-in-law-and-daughter-in-law friendship that succeeds, except when one of us is at her most impossible. She and Sam seem relaxed and bonded in parenting him today. We took turns playing with him, reading board books, handing him off to one another like a relay team.

We had cherries and apricots. There were white butterflies in the garden.

How could I have been okay imagining the three of them living in Chicago? Right now, I feel exactly the opposite. They belong here. Sam could finish school, and then I

301

could set him up in an inventor's dream laboratory. Amy could keep being a stay-at-home mom. So what if it would be hijacking their hero's journeys, and retard all three of them? So what if it would be like the psychic equivalent of Chinese footbinding? Sure, I might feel a tiny bit bad about that, but not as bad as I would feel if they moved across the country.

June 17

Jax is jibber-jabbering away, making word salad — language and communication put through a baby Cuisinart of babble.

His imitation of us really puts us in our place, knocks us down a peg or two: he hears this stuff that we think is so important, that we talk about all day, but he's giving back what he hears, and spewing it back at us, and it is gobbledygook.

He's so earnest about talking to us now, fully participating, saying: "I'm in the stream of life, too. Everything you can do with your mouths, I can do, too." I wonder if I was still okay when I was his age. If so, it wouldn't have been for long. I suspect that by age three, I had already been kidnapped by my parents' diseased marriage and returned, without anyone's knowing I'd been taken, seemingly intact, ready for a lifetime of polite anxiety and overachievement.

Jax's body and gestures are like ours, as he expresses things that have been zinging around his mind all these months. He can produce more grown-up sounds now, with intonation, emphasis, and question marks, instead of a monotone. This staggers the mind — from ticker tape to nuance in mere months.

"I'm part of the vertical world now," he's announcing. "I stand up, and hold on, I look you in the face, and I stare into your eyes, and then after a minute, breathy bubbly stuff with sound comes out of my mouth."

June 18

Jax can kiss now, openmouthed and ethereal, like an elderly sea anemone, or a bubble wand, or one of those pink chiffon octopuses that look like Eve Arden. His kisses leave a light film behind.

I took him out to lunch at a Mexican restaurant with a girlfriend today, and he was very easy, shoveling in massive amounts of avocado, plain beans, flour tortilla. But on the way home he pooped, and from the front seat it smelled like a sick walrus had gone to the bathroom in the backseat, or died. When I got home I laid him on my bed to change him, and said, "Wow, honey! This one is the new gold standard," and he clapped solemnly.

He pulls himself to his feet, holding on to table edges and chairs. He is going to walk any day, soon, maybe when Tom and I are in Europe next month. I told Sam and Amy, gently, "They don't walk *towards* you."

June 21, E-mail from Sam about Father's Day
This year was the first time I got to celebrate Father's Day as the father. In past years Father's Day has always been an improvised event. My mother isn't even a fan of Mother's Day, supposedly her big day, so creating a tradition for Father's Day was about experiment and imagination. I had great male mentors — my grandfather Rex, or Papa as I called him, who died when I was six; my uncles Stevo and John; the gay uncles; my Big Brother Brian; my adopted grandfather, Bill Tooley — and my mom and I always took the day to show love and thanks to the men in my life who looked after me and helped guide me on my journey, and still do. But I didn't get to do a heavily fatherly Father's Day with my dad, because I didn't meet him till I was seven, and I usually saw him only once a year, for

Thanksgiving week, so it was always make-shift.

Now I'm the dad, and Father's Day was a blank canvas for whatever I wanted to make of it. I woke up Sunday with a whole day full of plans, but that morning, none of them were what I wanted to do. All I wanted was to hang out with Jax all day, doing nothing, together. My mom always taught me that there was no shame in claiming a day completely for yourself, and informing everyone around you to be extra nice because it's your day. She would announce that it was International Anne Lamott Day, or Sam Lamott Day, and you got to call the shots, and you got to say your choice was to play catch or dinkum tennis in the driveway (me), or eat carrot cake frosting while watching disaster movies on TV (Mom). Amy was totally hands-on about doing all the unpleasant daily jobs so all that was left was pure guy time with Jax, my perfect hilarious little son.

I was really happy on Father's Day. I hung out with Amy and Jax, and it was great except for one thing. I wanted to talk with my dad. He and I had always done a pretty good job of staying in touch, but we hadn't talked in a few months — I was busy with Jax and school — and I was a little nervous to call. I had to leave a message for him, sort of discouragedly, but he called me back in fifteen minutes. We had a genuine conversation; it felt like the first time we were talking as two adults. We talked about how we were doing and what projects we were working on. I got a chance to tell him sincerely how grateful I was that we are in each other's lives and futures. I told him how our lost time together when I was young ended up playing such a huge part in my finding the strength and courage to stay in my son's life, no matter what. That's the most important fact of my life: that even though I was too young, and too terrified and confused, to be a dad, I promised God and Jax that I would show up and be the best father I could be.

The other important fact was that I got a clean slate with my father when I was young. So many kids I know were almost destroyed by being caught in the middle of the damage of their parents' drama, the parents hating or badmouthing each other. My life so far has been light-years away from the Disney images of families, but I wouldn't trade it, because getting to be a father, at the same time I get to have a relationship with my father, is such a blessing. I am getting to know Jax, my dad, and me all the time. What helped this happen was that my mom put me before herself, and had the class not to speak negatively of my dad while I was growing up, and she supported me and him in our relationship together, and that left a space for me to come up with my own opinions of him. He's odd and not perfect, but he has a big heart. He's unusual and very sensitive, which I grew up to be, which I hate — my mom is, too, so I got double-whammed. He and I have an understanding of how much we are to each other. We both mean really well, and we have both really screwed up. Nothing will ever change the fact that I had a single mother, but I forgave my father for the stuff or time he couldn't give me; I just dropped the bad feelings at some point. Well, you know, mostly.

Because, I mean, I have Jax, and having had my exact father helped give me that.

July 6

Sam, Amy, and Jax came over for a final Cousins dinner, to say good-bye, as I leave on vacation tomorrow. Tom and I are flying to England for a few days, and then we're taking a cruise ship to Eastern Europe with some sober friends. Besides Sam, Jax, Amy, we had Clara and Stevo, Neshama, Ricky and his girlfriend, who brought presents for Clara and Jax. Clara got colored pencils, and Jax got three crayons, tucked inside training crayon holders that look like gearshift knobs. He immediately ate part of the green crayon.

Our family was like a nutty circus in the living room. Ricky, who is tall and skinny like his father, is still mourning, but not acutely. We will all miss Millard forever. Clara drew with Jax. Amy sat next to him as he stood at the coffee table. I'm so glad Jax got her rich dark skin. She's lost at least half of her baby weight, but is still heavier than when she came to us. Three years ago, Amy was a size 00, and the parts of her were all struggling to hold together, after she had left her parents in North Carolina, her bigger family and best friends in Chicago. She and Sam were so in love, and they were between being kids and being adults. She was a full-time student at a cosmetology school in San Francisco, Sam was working full-time as a carpenter, making a living for both of them, while he waited to begin art school.

Now, a year after Jax, they have grown up: you see the utterly transformative effect of their becoming parents, even though their youthful appetites and wildness must still be a part of the mix. Amy is knit together by her focus on and love for Jax. But it is hard for her to feel whole, with so much of her heart two thousand miles away.

Stevo, and then Sam, tossed Jax in the air. This is such a guy thing — maybe it's like vertical football, or vertical catch. Anyhow, Jax laughs hysterically. He has an irresistible loose, silly laugh, like those Japanese cow noisemakers you tip over that make a metallic hiccup sound.

Neshama said later that Jax is the photographic negative of Sam as a baby — the dark hair and eyes and skin; all of towhead, fair, ethereal Sam's qualities spill out, spelled out with dark hair and olive skin.

They share deep powers of observation and focus, but Sam as a baby was more edgy in his watchfulness, while Jax has a sturdy, calm peasant quality.

Sam always had a solid workman's nature, and a plan, and Jax does, too: This is where this goes, we could shove *this* in here; now we should put this in our mouths, chew on it a minute, and now, on the count of three, fling.

Jax is unflappable, whereas Sam was quieter and reached for you like a koala bear, to watch from a safer post. Jax thrives in the midst of the Lamott family circus, with the big dogs lumbering around him, kissing him to within an inch of his life.

I try to stay with the delicious package of him, right here, right now. You have to keep looking at what you got right here: Jax, examining his universe methodically, centered and comfortable in his skin. He's busy exploring and inventing, moving things forward, fitting things together, then hauling himself up to a standing position, and clapping at his own prowess.

He's doing what a baby needs to do, to find out everything about life being lived around him, within his grasp and beyond. Our job, I guess, is simply to help keep him safe, support his explorations, and not have a complete collapse all the time from loving someone so deeply.

July 7

Tom and I flew to London today. We will spend a few days sightseeing with my cousin Robby, who is my age and has lived in London for ten years, and then fly to Stockholm with our friends for a cruise of the Baltic Sea. Tom got us upgrades to business class with the miles he has amassed by doing talks and workshops everywhere. He said that today would be about celebrating the twenty-fourth anniversary of my being clean and sober. That worked for me.

Our plane took off at two. We had a good meal, and he was acting like a semi-normal person for once: he had not said anything loud and awful about my heretical beliefs, or my butt, or how everyone on board is worried sick about me.

But at four, he dusted off his hands and said, "Your birthday is over now." When I protested, he tapped his watch and showed me its face. It was set to London time, where it was midnight. He went back to his book. I went back to mine.

July 9

Tom and Robby hit it off and were jabbering away a mile a minute about English history. I tagged along behind them like a Smurf. They are both brilliant students of history, and I could not keep up. However, I had the gum and a bottle of water, so they had to be nice to me.

In the Poets' Corner at Westminster Abbey, Tom especially wanted Robby to admire the marker of Gerard Manley Hopkins, whose poems Tom has been sending me for the twenty years that we have been friends. The epitaph over the monument is *"Esse quam videri,"* which Tom translated as "I am that I might see." His understanding was that it meant: "In order that I might see Life, with a capital L," as in the divine. He quoted Hopkins's famous lines: "The World is charged with the grandeur of God. / It will flame out, like shining from shook foil."

Robby asked, "What does that *mean?* I'm a Jew."

"It means that I might see the presence of God, the breath of God, the movement of God in our lives, the Love, the tasting of all of this. Hopkins is going beyond Annie's tense little friend Saint Paul, who wrote, 'Nothing can separate us from the love of God,' which was very radical at the time, because, well, it was Palestinians and Jews sitting down to lunch. These are the same people today. Paul was saying that everything connects us to love, like a tether. Whereas Hopkins addresses the *rhythm* of God — it goes fast, it goes slow, whatever. There's a heartbeat just beyond listening."

July 10

Stockholm is as fabulous and watery a city as Venice, fourteen islands set on a clean and expansive body of water. Who knew? I'm an American — we don't have to know this sort of thing. It is magical beyond words, medieval, mystical, friendly. I could stay here a long time. I went walking with my friend Ann, who was on the cruise, an old pal of Tom's. She can walk as fast and for as long as I can. Tom is good for an hour, max, so we left him behind. We crossed bridges from one island to the next, and saw castles, towers, parapets. At dusk, we asked a blond man — they're all blond — who jogged past us for instructions to the royal palace, and he shouted back to us over his shoulder, "No, no, free Swedish theater in the park! Free Swedish theater in the park!" We looked at each other, shrugged, and followed after him, until we came upon a great sprawling park, in the center of which was a stage surrounded by hundreds of people of all ages, babies and ancient old folks, too, many with picnics, who were watching an upbeat musical play unfold. The scene was Ingmar Bergman meets Abba. I ached for Jax to be there with me, up on my shoulders, clapping, babbling away in his native Swedish.

My annual herring needs were met midway by early evening.

Ann and I walked and walked until our feet ached; we were blissed out on the sights, the views, the people. But the best part of the visit was when I huddled alone with Tom before dinner. After my nap, we sat in the hotel lobby, looking at a catalogue of flowers that Tom would plant at his house and mine in the fall. He wanted me to pick out my favorite color daffodil for him to plant, but I said, "Don't they just die in four or five days, and not come until the following spring? So what is the point?"

"The point is those four or five days," he said.

July 12

Ann, Tom, and I spent today in Helsinki, trying to find shade from the heat wave in gorgeous and very orderly parks, then hiking to the great Uspenski Cathedral. It's a Finnish Orthodox church, built during the reign of Czar Alexander II, when Finland was part of the Russian empire. The outside is red brick with thirteen gilt onion-shaped domes, thirteen for Jesus and the twelve apostles. Inside, it's Romanesque arches and gold leaf everywhere, to inspire the same awe with which we will enter heaven. There's an ornate screen of painted wood, with angels, saints, even Saint John the Baptist holding his own head. Ow. It gave me a new perspective on the mild headache I have had for a couple of days. Above and behind the screen is a marvelous deep blue dome ceiling with stars, like a medieval planetarium, and screens to protect the priests from the sight of us while they conduct services, because we on this side are too revolting for words; I certainly felt this today, fat and sweaty, with a limp like a clubfoot, from a blister. Tom looked, as usual, like a wino hippie, wearing a Mexican wedding shirt and an expensive Australian hat.

The art was Byzantine — all icons and saints, which Tom said was very fourth- and fifth-century, all the gold paint, the intricate mosaics, the hammered silver over small oil paintings. I got mesmerized, lost Tom briefly, and wandered around in the corners and clusters of tourists like Quasimodo looking for Esmeralda. I finally found Tom outside, talking with a man who was a chemist from Holland, about — as Tom put it to him — this business of God.

Tom was explaining the Nicene Creed to the chemist: God the Father is the creator of everything, physical and invisible; the Son becomes incarnate, suffers, dies, and is risen; and the Holy Spirit "proceeds" from the Father. Everything was fine, until Charlemagne came along and wanted to emphasize one radical word: *filioque,* which means "and from the son," i.e., the Holy Spirit proceeds from the Father and the Son, instead of just from the Father.

And then the shit hit the fan.

The Greek Orthodox Church maintained that this was change, therefore heretical. The Latin Church thought of it as clarification. Everyone became fanatical, and if you disagreed with other people's understanding, then they got to kill you. This is all very modern, very Sarah Palin.

The chemist asked Tom where he stood, and Tom quoted the great Cardinal Newman, who described the truth of the risen Christ as a huge shining diamond above everything else. But every so often, Tom said, because life is change, the light changes and we see things differently. And to paraphrase Pope John Paul II, you say potato, I say potahto, and not everyone has to see things exactly the same way. Tom said that either you learn to live with paradox and ambiguities, or you'll be six years old for the rest of your life. Tom and the chemist shook hands warmly, and we limped off with Ann to the open-air market, where the raspberries were the size of aggies.

I wondered if raspberries were still Jax's favorite food, along with grapes and peas. I wrote texts and e-mails to Sam and Amy, but didn't hear back. I imagined the worst: jails, foster care, both dogs dead.

July 13

I thought about Jax in every port and every town, like a bad song. He's my little soldier boy. The word *pining* came to mind. I wondered what new things he has learned to do. I was medium pissed that Sam and Amy had dropped off the radar, and I decided that I would not get them the great presents I had intended to. This is how we Christians do things.

Today we were in Saint Petersburg for eighteen hours, and it was pretty great — the Hermitage, several of the world's great cathedrals, the Summer Palace, which is what Liberace would have overseen if he'd been a dictator, and a night of ballet — *Giselle.* But even better than all those gold onion-shaped domes, grand parks, and the harbor was the cab ride Ann and I took from the ballet to the ship.

We agreed on a price of twenty dollars American, for what would turn out to be a ten-minute ride, which was fine. The cabbie knew only ten words of English, including "twenty dollars American" and "I loves Obama." His name was Akman, and he was Armenian, swarthy and fat, with thick stubble, and he chain-smoked Luckys. He was like someone sent over by central casting to play the fat, swarthy Armenian with stubble. Every few minutes, Ann, Akman, or I shouted out, "I love Obama!" and we'd all clap enthusiastically, like Jax. Until we arrived at the docks. Then he tried to rip us off — twenty dollars *each,* he now said. Bad feelings erupted, and we gave him one twenty-dollar bill and started to storm off, feeling like embittered capitalist pigs. Then we heard the window roll down, and held our breaths — was he going to shoot us? Instead, Akman shouted, "I loves Obama!" and we shouted that we did, too, and all three of us clapped and I raised my fists in the power salute. "Thank you, my friends!" he shouted, holding his hands over his heart, pure love on his face, like Jesus in His distressing guise as a fat, swarthy cabbie with five-o'clock shadow.

It's wonderful to travel again when the rest of the world does not feel that war criminals are in charge of your country.

July 15

Ann and I left the ship and walked all day. Riga, the capital of Latvia, is the loveliest city of gardens, towers, bridges, and random daisies everywhere. Tom was too tired and cranky to leave the ship, so he wasn't along as our guide. Consequently, all we had to go on as we made our way around town were ten postcards I bought from a peddler — we were like gentle space aliens who'd landed in Latvia on a peaceful mission. We stopped people, showed them a postcard of a church or a cathedral, of the great public garden along the canal, of monuments of the Viking trade routes, of the statue of freedom, and they pointed us in the right direction. We walked along the lively ancient streets to the river, where we stopped to watch a cross-eyed calico cat chase white butterflies. He had a bright red nose, like a clown, and he was a great hunter. We watched for quite a long time in the shade of some trees, out of the heat. He didn't actually catch any butterflies, possibly because he was so cross-eyed. But just as we were about to leave, with a sudden furry *grand jeté,* he brought down a purple-blue lilylike blossom, an agapanthus, and wrestled it to the ground. Ann and I cheered, like it was an Olympic event.

Maybe it was the heat and the exhaustion, but at that moment I had a revelation: One of our best family friends grew agapanthus in a corner of the unfenced garden in front of her house, and she got so tired of boys' taking shortcuts through her garden and tromping on her flowers that she had a housepainter make a sign that she stuck into the ground. It read: "Beware the Agapan-thus."

I realized, in that moment, that almost all the things I had feared and dreaded my whole life had been like those agapanthus, not threatening at all, except in the imagination of a confused young girl whose parents had a bad marriage.

We went back to the ship by way of the Latvian freedom monument that separates the old town from the newer city, a tall, slender copper woman atop a high column, holding three gilded stars.

July 16

In Poland, I did not decide to visit Stutthof, the concentration camp, until the very last moment. It felt like there was something obscene about taking a tour bus to see a Nazi camp, the first built outside Germany and the last to be liberated. But Tom had been to Auschwitz, and he thought it might be important for me to go and observe, to get at a cellular level the fact that despite our great love and art, we are a violent species. Cain is still killing Abel, and that was meaningful for people like me, who can write to bear witness, remind others of this in the hopes of preventing such madness in the future.

Another woman from our sober group, Keenan, went with me — Tom was going to the Solidarity shrines on his own — and she and I stuck close together, huddling on the tour bus like schoolgirls. She is a Presbyterian minister, a compassionate soul; we did not talk much, only to admit that being on a tour bus with a friend, ludicrous as it might seem, was the only way either of us would have ever seen a concentration camp.

I loved our guide, a smart, no-nonsense, but gentle Polish woman, who took us first to the Solidarity shrines. Then, after an hour's ride out to the beautiful countryside, there was a long drive through woods. Keenan and I were both anxious the whole time, knowing that right around the corner would be the gates of the camp. You can't gear up for its sudden, stark appearance.

The blackness and bleakness and unreality of Stutthof hit you like the heat. We stepped through the gates into the ultimate harshness, hearts sinking. A storage cabin held tens of thousands of pairs of shoes, every single pair of shoes a fully formed human life, and over a sign, baby shoes hung by their laces. I stopped to take it in, and fell in with a tall older Swede named David who had also dropped back from the rest of the group. He teared up at the display of baby shoes, but by that point I actually felt next to nothing. We entered an oppressive scrunched warren of living quarters, barracks, and walked in a daze through the horror of the "hospital" rooms. I felt terrible studying the enlarged photographs of the victims on the walls and at the wrenching reality of how many children had been murdered, but I plodded along like a robot, staying close to Keenan and David. I wanted the tour to be over, wanted to be back on the bus and able to say sadly for now and all time that I had seen one of the camps.

A quiet expanse of dark yard lay in the middle of the camp — on one side were the barracks and hospital, on the other was the museum display, mostly photos and newspaper clippings. On the walls, monstrous memorabilia in cases. David's face was in deep grief; Keenan seemed to be in overwhelmed, puzzled wretchedness. We were shown to the crematorium, to the left of the museum, where the smell of ashes remains. The two small ovens were almost hideously lovely, like appliances you might buy at IKEA, miserably human. I couldn't leave that room. I do not know what was going on inside me, but I kept sneaking back while everyone else went on to the next exhibit. The nearby gas chamber was rather small

322

and innocuous, until you looked up and saw the hole in the ceiling for the can of Zyklon B. Upon seeing this hole, there is not one helpful thought you can think.

Our group had moved on to a beautiful meadow behind the crematorium, where one set of gallows remained. I caught up to David in the shade of a grove of silver trees. Keenan was bending down low to look at wildflowers. I couldn't remember what kind of trees they were, although we have them where I live. David did not know the word in English, but he drew the picture of the leaf on my sheath of notes, and he wrote the word for them in Swedish, *björk.* He told me how, in the fall, the leaf drops off, and the new bud is already in place, fully formed but tiny, waiting to be born again in spring.

David, Keenan, and I trundled back to the bus like refugees.

When we got back on board, Keenan shared a bright, juicy mandarin orange with me.

The shoes, the ovens, the gas chamber, the faces in the photographs, the meadow with the leafless trees, Christ crucified and waiting to be reborn again; I could not make sense of anything, except that by the time we got back to Gdansk, I remembered the name of the tree in English: silver birch.

July 17

It was our last full day on board, and we had docked in Visby, Sweden, in the pouring rain. Early tomorrow we would cruise into Stockholm, and later I would fly home. Tom and I found each other in a secret corner of the dining room and had breakfast together. I had my usual girly healthy balanced breakfast, and Tom had eggs, potatoes, and three different kinds of fatty carcinogenic pork products. After our usual catch-up and gossip, I looked up and asked, "Can I tell you everyone I hate?" He nodded, and put down his fork, as if this were confession.

I told him about a couple of exes who still vex me, and one with whom I had hoped to get back together, and how much I still hated what my parents' terrible marriage had saddled my brothers and me with; and about two women who were formerly in our family, who behaved beyond heinously in their divorces from beloved family members; and about everything Sam and Amy had done wrong over the year, beginning prenatally, up to and including not staying in touch with me now, and how awful they could be to each other, in front of Jax, and what an entitled white male Sam could be sometimes with both me and Amy, and how

324

impossible and bullheaded she could be; a few random writers who have been mean to me, and of course, entire presidential administrations.

I heaved a sigh and stared down into my lap, done, for the time being.

"Let me get us more coffee and some pastry," he said. "We need communion."

When he got back, I told him about how I had pinched Sam really hard on the arm once. Tom handed me half a glazed doughnut. "I hate that I'm so crazy, and shut down, all at once. I hate that I love Sam so much, the same way I love Jesus. Maybe it would have been healthier if I'd had more kids."

"Well, yeah, you love him," Tom said. "He's the son." I'd never thought of that. He continued, "Even Joseph and Mary must have been beside themselves half the time, with this strange, strange kid of theirs."

"Do you think God, the Father, was terrified for Jesus?"

"Well, at least concerned."

"And what do you do in the face of this powerlessness? As a parent?"

"You get to be obsessed and angry," Tom said. "And they get to be the age they are, and act like teenagers if they want to. There is a zero-percent chance you will change them. So we breathe in, and out, talk to friends, as needed. We show up, wear clean underwear, say hello to strangers. We plant bulbs, and pick up litter, knowing there will be more in twenty minutes. We pray that we might cooperate with *any* flicker of light we can find in the world."

Later, Ann and I disembarked, but it was raining too hard for a walk, and I ended up in bed; at first I felt lonely, tired, peeved with Sam and Amy, maybe a little more lost than usual, but soon I got lost in a good way, with a book, which is also to get found, and my staunchest lifelong light.

July 19

Yesterday our ship arrived in Stockholm harbor at dawn. Tom and our friends were going to spend a couple more days in the city, but I headed directly to the airport, and was back in San Francisco in the evening. Jax and Amy and Sam were here to welcome me home. I am hosting Jax's birthday party tomorrow. Everyone who is anyone will be here. Jax was shy with me for approximately four seconds: maybe Bonnie is right, that our love for each other is indelible, and not based on proximity — she has promised me this. He threw himself into my arms, tucked his head under my neck, like a dove. He is very grown-up, scooching around his fiefdom to take possession of anything within reach, and trying to fend off the kissing dogs, who want to clean him every five minutes, like geishas. He's such a mellow, peaceful guy, busy bashing my things against the floor or coffee table. He reaches for one of us from time to time, and lets us hold him until he wiggles and wants to get back down so he can pick up things and fling them about. Sam and Amy seem to be in semi-okay shape, friendly enough, and civil, so blown away in love with my guy, Smash Crasher, who blithely goes on about his work.

The three of them put me to bed at eight. Sam actually tucked me in. Jax was instructed to give me several jellyfish kisses, which he did, and they tiptoed out.

July 20

I woke up at five this morning in a fog of headache and Komodo dragon breath: both dogs standing over me on the bed, watching for the first signs of life, their heads maybe a foot away from mine. When my eyes flickered, trying to focus, they peered at me wildly, like maybe the house was on fire. Or I should get up so the dogs and I could start pulling things together for Jax's one-year birthday. Or else they were hungry, which I was, too.

One year old already. I can't really get my mind around this. It passed in many paces and timbres, like an opera. I got up to feed the dogs and the kitty, and felt like hell with jet lag. I made a list in my head of all the things I had to do: find enough forks for twenty, remember where I put the festive plates and napkins with cupcakes on them, pick up the wreckage Jax and his slovenly no-goodnik parents had left behind, sneak in a short granny nap.

Sam, Amy, and Jax came over early, before the party. People weren't coming till five. Jax chattered away about arrangements. He definitely knows what's he saying now — he has laid out certain work for himself to do, and he talks away, as you should know about it all, because his work and discoveries are so fascinating. The only actual words are "Dada," "Mama," "Nana," a generalized *d* sound for dog, "duhhy," and for the kitty cat, "ditty dah." Yet he's very assured, no longer simply playing with sounds, but expressing himself. He's grown from a helpless newborn to an accomplished and complex human being who is days away from walking. He's grown me, too: grandchildren grow you. With your own child, you're fixated on the foreground, trying to keep the child safe and alive. But with a grandchild, you can be in softer focus, you can see beyond the anxious foreground. Jax is absolutely nutty, like the rest of us, fluent, and fluid like a stream, with lightness, richness, silkiness, stones: echoes, undertones, overtones, melodies, whining, burbling; cool water flowing, pinging, and roaring past pebbles and plants and its own clear self.

ACKNOWLEDGMENTS

Thank you, Sam and Amy, for letting me tell this story. Thank you, Jake Morrissey, for being the ideal editor and friend. Thank you, Riverhead, especially Anna Jardine, Mih-Ho Cha, Ali Cardia, and Craig Burke. I love all the publicity people, both hardcover and paperback. They make me feel loved and safe. Thank you, St. Andrew Presbyterian Church of Marin City: You are my favorite place in the world.

ABOUT THE AUTHORS

Anne Lamott is the author of the *New York Times* bestsellers *Grace (Eventually), Plan B, Traveling Mercies,* and *Operating Instructions,* as well as several novels, including *Imperfect Birds* and *Rosie*. A past recipient of a Guggenheim Fellowship and an inductee to the California Hall of Fame, she lives in Northern California.

Sam Lamott is an inventor, designer, entrepreneur, and artist who lives in San Francisco.

The employees of Thorndike Press hope you have enjoyed this Large Print book. All our Thorndike, Wheeler, and Kennebec Large Print titles are designed for easy reading, and all our books are made to last. Other Thorndike Press Large Print books are available at your library, through selected bookstores, or directly from us.

For information about titles, please call:
(800) 223-1244

or visit our Web site at:
http://gale.cengage.com/thorndike

To share your comments, please write:
Publisher
Thorndike Press
10 Water St., Suite 310
Waterville, ME 04901